Selves and Others

Selves and Others
exploring language and identity

Myles Holloway
Gwen Kane
Riana Roos
Michael Titlestad

EDUCATIONAL CONSULTANTS   Finuala Dowling
Alice Goodwin-Davey
Dennis Walder

ADDITIONAL MATERIAL BY   Deirdre Byrne
Karen Scherzinger
Becky Simmonds

CAPE TOWN
OXFORD UNIVERSITY PRESS
1999

Oxford University Press

Great Clarendon Street, Oxford OX2 6DP, United Kingdom

offices in
Oxford, New York
Athens, Auckland, Bangkok, Bogotá, Buenos Aires, Calcutta, Cape Town
Chennai, Dar es Salaam, Delhi, Florence, Hong Kong, Istanbul, Karachi
Kuala Lumpur, Madrid, Melbourne, Mexico City, Mumbai, Nairobi, Paris
São Paulo, Singapore, Taipei, Tokyo, Toronto, Warsaw

and associated companies in
Berlin, Ibadan

OXFORD is a registered trademark of Oxford University Press

Selves and Others: exploring language and identity

ISBN 0 19 571683 3
© University of South Africa 1999

First published 1999

EDITOR: Arthur Attwell
DESIGNER: Mark Standley

Published by Oxford University Press Southern Africa
PO Box 12119, N1 City, 7463, Cape Town, South Africa

Set in 10.5 pt on 14 pt Minion
Reproduction by RHT desktop publishing cc, Durbanville
Cover reproduction by RJH Graphic Reproduction, Cape Town
Printed and bound by Creda Communications, Eliot Avenue,
Eppindust II, Cape Town, South Africa

Contents

Introduction

SELVES AND OTHERS: EXPLORING LANGUAGE AND IDENTITY is concerned with meaning and interpretation in one language: English. Language is at the heart of human understanding and experience. Without language, human society as we know it would not exist. Languages, as systems of signs, give us ways to codify experience and communicate it among people across time, space and culture. Any language is a powerful tool used by its speakers to make sense of their worlds and to interact with each other. Moreover, languages allow us to deal with things without their being real or physically observable. For instance, we can talk about fairies even though they don't exist, or atoms without seeing them. With language we can create new worlds and aspire towards states of knowing, seeing and being that are limited only by the extent of our imaginations.

Selves and Others is aimed at students who are beginning an advanced study of English at university or college. It provides a framework within which some aspects of English language and literature can be considered. We focus on various themes and issues, and ask:

- ✪ How do we make sense of the world around us, particularly in relation to the words we use?
- ✪ What role do people play in giving things their meanings?
- ✪ How do we know that our interpretations of meaning are reliable?
- ✪ How do we process our interpretations and shape them in purposeful and socially significant ways?

These are by no means the only questions that arise when we consider the world, the ways in which it is interpreted and our representations of its meanings. We also do not want to suggest that these questions can be answered easily, or that this book will provide neat formulas that can be learnt and applied to life or to literature. *Selves and Others* is not a blueprint outlining answers. Rather, it is the starting point from which we, as teachers and learners, can begin a voyage of exploration and discovery.

Our journey starts with ourselves. Chapter one – 'Autobiography: Exploring "The Self"' – looks closely at the idea of 'the self' and how a person's identity is revealed in autobiographical writing. A central question here is what role language plays in creating the unique identities that we believe each and every person possesses.

In chapter two – 'Characterization: People and Perspectives' – the focus of the book widens when we use the insights we have gained from our exploration of autobiographical identity to explore the characters of other people. Humans are social creatures: we live in communities with other people. Social interaction relies on our being able to interpret clues in the behaviour and words of the people we encounter both face-to-face and in what we read.

Chapter three – 'Made for Each Other: Ideas about Gender' – looks at the relationship between language, writing and gender. This chapter focuses particularly on how women are defined and interpreted; it asks whether meaning is influenced by gender and whether we interpret things in specific ways because of gender. The chapter discusses some of the ways in which attitudes and assumptions about gender affect how we think about texts and people.

Chapter four – 'Writing Worlds Apart: Representing Culture' – continues our journey by exploring the relationship between culture and meaning. Here the focus is on how we respond to and interpret groups of people who differ from us. This chapter suggests that the ways in which we speak and write about people reveal what we think about them. It also asks us to consider how much our representations of other cultures may be projections of our own ideas and identity.

At the centre of this book is a key question: to what extent do objects, actions, and ideas possess an inherent meaning, and to what extent is meaning something that humans create? This is a question that has occupied scholars for centuries, so don't be surprised that we can write an entire book without answering it. In broad terms we can identify two extreme positions. On the one hand, it could be argued that things have an inherent and natural meaning. Footprints, for instance, would still appear behind us even if we never turned around and noticed them. They exist independently of being named and can be separated from language. Even if we did not have words for them they would continue to exist and to indicate something: 'someone has been here'. On the other hand, it has been argued that meaning is something that is imposed on or written into things. We do not notice our footprints until we can differentiate them from the ground, and we can only differentiate them when we have words for them, when we can say 'that's ground, and that's footprint'. According to this argument, language comes before things; it is only through words that things exist, and we cannot conceive of reality 'outside' of language. Most modern thinkers hold views that exist somewhere on the spectrum between these two extremes.

The writers of this book explore the possibility that meaning is not always something that is fixed, certain or unchanging. They look at circumstances in which meanings may be fluid and debatable. They ask: is meaning a construction, shaped by language, context and perspective? Does meaning have a social basis? Do the possibilities of meaning shift as time passes and societies change? If the answers to these questions are 'yes', then the meanings that we attribute to things (including texts and ideas) are provisional. They exist only until they are proved untrue, until they become unfashionable, or until they are replaced by new sets of associations, denotations and connotations.

It would be dishonest for a book that suggests that meaning is variable to insist on its own correctness. If the meanings that things have are difficult to define and to pinpoint, then what we say in this book is also open to interpretation and discussion. *Selves and Others* should not be read as a voice of authority that cannot be challenged. This is not a book that intends to speak down to its readers. Instead, in it we hope to establish a conversation between its writers and its readers.

Conversation – the exchange of ideas in a process of mutual discovery – depends on the participants being willing to speak and to listen. This book has been written with the idea in mind that learning should affirm our sense of self-worth and enhance our independence and dignity as human beings; through learning we can change our lives for the better. The writers see this process of learning (and, therefore, this book) as an opportunity for co-operation, and as a space in which we share ideas in pursuit of new discoveries. Both writers and readers can benefit from this journey. Learners can gain from the experience of teachers, and teachers see themselves and their teaching in new ways through the eyes of their learners.

Discovery, dialogue and sharing are built into the structure of *Selves and Others*. The book has been written to begin with familiar concepts and to move gradually into areas that are new, and where the ideas may be more and more challenging. Each chapter in the book follows this pattern, as does each section of each chapter. Throughout the book we start by establishing what we know already. Once we are clear about our current position and understanding, we can take a step into the unknown. New ideas unravel before us, and through questioning, discussion, investigation and research we become familiar with the unfamiliar.

A dialogue means that we will not merely receive or convey passively a volume of information. Instead we will have to state our own opinions and draw on our own experiences. You will see as you read the book that as writers we have not been afraid to let our personalities show in the chapters we have written. Where we think we can best illustrate an idea by letting the personal identity of one of the writers emerge, that has happened. At times you will notice that we write as 'we', at times as 'I'. The 'I' is not always the same person, since the four chapters were written by different people.

The need for the reader's active involvement in the learning process is also clear from the way in which the writers ask questions rather than simply make statements. Sometimes these questions are signalled by directions, such as *Time off ... to think!* At other times they appear as part of the general flow of the text. Here are three examples of the kind of questions we ask and the format in which you will see them:

✪ In your experience, what has the study of English involved?

✪ Why are you studying English? And what do you hope to gain from your studies?

✪ How do you think this book will differ from or be similar to what you expect English studies to be like?

There are no 'right' answers to these questions. Like many that we ask, they simply require your opinion or a statement of what you currently know. In these questions *what* you think is less important than the fact that you *do* think.

Where we would like you to consider particular ideas, we offer help. This might take the form of a direct statement of our interpretation. If we were to offer guidance on the questions about English studies, for example, we would tell you that in our experience courses in English have tended to study language and literature separately. Literary studies, in turn, have often focused on the technical aspects of writing, such as explaining imagery or irony. By contrast, *Selves and Others* integrates the study of language and of literature. Instead of focusing on literary techniques, we grapple with broad issues, all concerned with meaning and interpretation in a variety of fields.

Thinking and questioning are often more difficult than we expect, especially when the subject of investigation is as subtle as a language and its literature. To assist you, we have added labels and notes to our central narrative and to some of the pieces of writing we want you to read. We have also put a °symbol after certain words. The meanings of these words can be found in the Glossary at the back of this book.

Another important part of this book is its information boxes, which look like the one on page xii. These expand our thinking by providing additional information on the topic being discussed. They also offer small steps sideways into areas that run parallel to the issues at hand. Alongside the main text, the information boxes provoke new sets of associations and new areas for discovery. One way to use these information boxes to extend your understanding in an area is to refer to an encyclopedia. You could also use the topics they raise in a subject search in a library catalogue, or, if you have access to an on-line computer, as keywords in a search machine on the Internet.

HOW BIG IS THE ENGLISH LANGUAGE?

The English vocabulary has increased enormously since the Middle Ages. The most comprehensive English dictionary – the *Oxford English Dictionary* – contains 500 000 entries. Estimates suggest that at present the English language contains over a million words, including slang expressions, words from various dialects and scientific or technical terms. This makes English the language with the largest vocabulary. One of the reasons for this is that English has borrowed words from almost every major European language (such as Latin, French or Greek) and from many other languages (such as Afrikaans and Malay).

Learning is a never-ending, life-long activity. To this end, *Selves and Others* must be read in conjunction with other books. Your interaction with this book should be part of your interaction with a whole range of texts – literary and non-literary. Use the ways of thinking you develop in this book whenever you read a poem, play or novel. Look at television, movies and advertisements in the light of the ideas you find here. Consider the things you have thought about here whenever you listen to a political speech, read a newspaper article or have a discussion with friends. Draw on the ideas and questions outlined in this book in your everyday (non-academic) life and in your relationships with other people. This is a book that can make it possible for you to think about yourself and your world in new and exciting ways.

Selves and Others

1 Autobiography: Exploring 'The Self'

IN THIS CHAPTER you are going to be thinking and writing about yourself as an individual. Your main purpose will be to introduce yourself, to define who you are and what is important about you. We will explore ideas about identity and the ways in which people present that identity to others, especially in writing. The chapter begins by discussing the concept of 'the self' and by considering some of the ways in which people represent themselves. It then looks at excerpts from Nelson Mandela's autobiography, *Long Walk to Freedom*, before ending with a section in which you will write your own autobiographical piece.

KNOW THYSELF
  Socrates

I THINK, THEREFORE I AM
  Descartes

I AM WHAT I AM AND WHAT I AM NEEDS NO EXCUSES
  Gloria Gaynor

. . . .

1 Why am I important? or Why is what I am important?

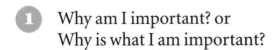

Who we are is vitally important for how we relate to other people and to the world around us. Our personal identity is the basis for all our physical and emotional interactions. Using ourselves as a point of departure when viewing the world is something that human beings cannot escape. Whether we speak about things that are as unrelated as tall buildings, the future of marriage, political trends in South Africa, or small changes in temperature, everything we say and think comes from a point in time and space that is unique to us as individuals.

ONE

PERSONAL MEANING

Think about yourself and answer these questions:
- ✪ What makes you a human being?
- ✪ How are you different from other people?
- ✪ What makes you special as a person?

The capacity for self-knowledge and self-reflection° (which you have just demonstrated in answering these questions) may be the characteristic that defines us as human and separates us from other species. An important aspect of the human species, which you may have mentioned in your answers, is humankind's ability to use the tool of language. Language is the means by which we make sense of ourselves and our world, because it's only by naming things that we can order them in ways that have meaning. Look at these photographs:

Can you know or describe the difference between the things in the photographs without words?

How do words empower us to make sense of things? Language allows individuals to communicate and to interact in ways that are understood by other people. Using a language means using specific sounds and signs according to a code° that is accepted and understood by a particular community of users. In this book, the code we are using has a name, it's called the English language.

More than three hundred million people worldwide use this code, English, as their main language, while as many as a billion people can speak, read or write it. This means that about one fifth of the world's population can represent themselves in English.

The study of English, then, is the study of how people who use this global code represent themselves in relation to each other and the world.

People's representations of themselves or of the world around them are sometimes highly complex, formal expressions. In the case of poetry, for instance, the poet may use symbols to refer to feelings and ideas. An example of a symbol would be using a dove to represent peace, or a rose to suggest love. The language of the poem is likely to be tightly structured and may be carefully planned to fit patterns of rhythm and rhyme. The writer may also have deliberately experimented with variations of sound through a certain choice of words (and by changes in word order) to communicate a specific message or suggest various ideas.

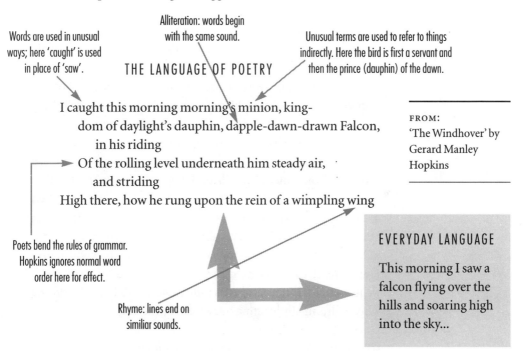

Words are used in unusual ways; here 'caught' is used in place of 'saw'.

Alliteration: words begin with the same sound.

Unusual terms are used to refer to things indirectly. Here the bird is first a servant and then the prince (dauphin) of the dawn.

THE LANGUAGE OF POETRY

I caught this morning morning's minion, king-
dom of daylight's dauphin, dapple-dawn-drawn Falcon, in his riding
Of the rolling level underneath him steady air,
and striding
High there, how he rung upon the rein of a wimpling wing

FROM:
'The Windhover' by
Gerard Manley
Hopkins

Poets bend the rules of grammar. Hopkins ignores normal word order here for effect.

Rhyme: lines end on similiar sounds.

EVERYDAY LANGUAGE

This morning I saw a falcon flying over the hills and soaring high into the sky...

But even less formal, everyday language can be complex. There are situations in which you would use a more formal type of language (and behaviour) than in other circumstances. For example, lectures, religious addresses, political speeches and job interviews all demand a particular kind of language use. Imagine that you are discussing your prospects for promotion with the chief executive of the company for which you work. Think about the following questions:

- ✪ How would you dress for the interview?
- ✪ How would you sit?
- ✪ Would you use the chief executive's first name? Why or why not?
- ✪ Would the chief executive call you by your first name? Why do you think so?
- ✪ Would you speak to the chief executive formally or informally?
- ✪ Now think about how different the meeting would be if you were talking to a junior employee who works under you. You are now the boss. What would change? How?

Your discussion with the chief executive is likely to follow certain unspoken rules and conventions° (for example, you probably won't swear or pick your nose during the discussion). You will adopt a specific tone and attitude, which will be indicated both by your choice of words and by the way in which they are delivered. You may even adopt a particular way of standing or sitting in order to show that you acknowledge the authority your boss has over you. Significantly, much of what you do and how you behave will be unconscious. You will probably take it for granted that speaking and behaving in this way are natural and normal, when in fact your behaviour and use of language might be learnt, in other words, they might be conditioned° and socialized°.

But before we look at some of the ways in which people represent themselves – in language and life, formally and informally – we need to look at ourselves as individuals. Let's begin by stating who we are and by locating ourselves in time and space.

MY NAME:	I am Myles Holloway.
WHERE I AM IN TIME:	I am writing this on 16 January 1998.
WHERE I AM IN SPACE:	I am in my study at home in Johannesburg, Gauteng, South Africa.

Now do the same for yourself.

NAME: I am ...
DATE: I am working through this chapter on ...
LOCATION: I am in/at ...

In these statements you have taken a step towards representing yourself autobiographically: you have asserted an aspect of your identity. These statements have also established a particular relationship between you, me and this chapter. The reason for locating yourself in relation to this chapter and this book is straightforward: you are an active participant in the learning process°. Just as you are at the centre of all your experiences, you are also the focus of this learning experience. As such, learning is not just about receiving knowledge. It is also about making that knowledge personally valuable. Your viewpoint is important. At each stage of this book, you will be actively involved in making your own learning meaningful to yourself.

See pages i –x in your *Oxford Advanced Learner's Dictionary* for further explanations of how to read and use a dictionary.

 2 Who do you see when you look into the mirror?

Before we go on to write more fully about ourselves, let's first see how a dictionary can help to explain what an autobiography is.

This tells us the plural form of the word.

Words in bold are known as headwords. They are arranged alphabetically.

Meanings of words are separated by numbers. When the meanings are closely related, letters are used.

auto /'ɔːtəʊ/ *n* (*pl* **-os**) (*infml esp US*) a car. *the auto industry.*
aut(o)- *comb form* **1** of oneself: *autobiography* ○ *autograph.* **2** by oneself or itself; independent(ly): *autocracy* ○ *automobile.*
autobiography /ˌɔːtəbaɪ'ɒgrəfi/ *n* (**a**) [C] the story of a person's life written by that person: *A more detailed account of the incident is given in her autobiography.* (**b**) [U] this type of writing. Compare BIOGRAPHY.
   ▶ **autobiographical** /ˌɔːtəˌbaɪə'græfɪkl/ *adj* of or concerning autobiography: *His novels are largely autobiographical* (ie They describe many of his own experiences).
autocracy /ɔː'tɒkrəsi/ *n* (**a**) [U] government of a country by one person with absolute power. (**b**) [C] a country governed in this way.

An abbreviation which indicates the part of speech (in this case, a noun).

A word that is related to the word being defined. Look up this word for further information.

Indicates whether the noun is (C) countable or (U) uncountable.

The meaning of the word.

How the word is used.

Phonetic symbols indicate how words are pronounced.

The word 'autobiography' comes from three Greek words, *autos*, which means 'self', *bios*, which means 'life', and *grapho*, which means 'to write'. Literally, then, an autobiography is the 'story of one's life written by one's self'.

Most stories share certain characteristics. For instance, they tend to have a beginning, a middle and an end; they are set in specific places and times; and they are told from a particular point of view or perspective°. When you write an autobiography, you are writing about yourself and your experiences from your perspective.

Writing about yourself without using your name involves using the personal pronouns 'I' and 'me'. These pronouns are among the simplest ways of referring to yourself. In other words, they are the primary means of self-reference. When you are the subject of your reference, you use the pronoun 'I'. However, when you refer to yourself as the object of your sentence you use 'me'. The pronouns 'I' and 'me' indicate different relationships between you and the world. Let's look at some sentences which use the word 'I':

✪ I am studying English.
✪ This morning I shot an elephant in my pyjamas .
✪ I hope to write the most important novel of the century.

In each of these sentences the word 'I' is the subject. As the subject, 'I' indicates the person who is performing an action or who is in a particular condition. In other words, the speaker is doing or experiencing the action or condition expressed in the sentence. The sentences themselves are expressions which describe or characterize the subject. If you had written the sentences above, they would tell your reader something about you.

Describe yourself in more detail by completing the following sentences.

I AM ...

I LIKE ...

AT THIS MOMENT I AM FEELING ...   BECAUSE ....

Some would say that the fact that we use the capital letter 'I' instead of the small letter 'i' to refer to ourselves in English indicates the importance that we grant to ourselves as people. Individual identity and consciousness of the self is possible only through showing how we are different from other people. We cannot think or speak of being an 'I' unless we can separate the 'I' from someone who is not 'I'; in other words, unless we can think of a 'you'. The world population is approximately 5,3 billion. Every one of these 5,3 billion people has the right to use the pronoun 'I' (or the equivalent, if there is one, in their own language). Whenever we say 'I' we are explicitly separating ourselves from all other people. This may seem obvious, but it is a crucial point. Being aware of the concept 'I' is the first step towards establishing an individual identity.

Another way in which we separate ourselves from all the others who are entitled to use the word 'I' is through the use of proper nouns or specific names.

The proper nouns that I use for myself are Myles Kenton Holloway. My names set me apart from people who do not have the same name as I do. They might also tell someone who didn't know me certain things about me. I am probably a male – I have names that are usually given to boys. I may be English-speaking, because my names sound English. Finally, my name suggests that I had parents who liked slightly unusual names.

Of course, my name does not give you much information about me. The person I am is not fully described by my name since it gives very little information about my physical being – you may, as I pointed out above, realize from my name that I have a male body, but the name will tell you nothing else about my body. Similarly, my name says nothing about my psychological identity. My inner life is not described at all by my name since it reveals nothing about my feelings, ideas, beliefs and experiences. There is no necessary connection between my name and my physical or psychological identity. In fact, the connection between who I am and my name is a matter of convention°. I am Myles Kenton Holloway because my parents gave me that name, and other people have agreed to use it when referring to me.

THE POET e. e. cummings often used lower-case letters where we would normally use capitals. He especially preferred using 'i' instead of 'I' to make his readers think about the significance we attach to ourselves. He even insisted that his own name be spelled with lower-case letters. This is one of his poems:

Who are you,little i

(five or six years old)
peering from some high

window;at the gold

of november sunset

(and feeling:that if day
has to become night

this is a beautiful way)

FROM: *The New Yorker Book of Poems.* 1974. New York: William Morrow & Co.

● IF YOU had been given a different name when you were born from the one you were given, how would it have influenced your life?

People have learnt that this name is associated with me. I could change my name to Jabu Ndlovu and as long as other people agreed to refer to me by this name, I would be Jabu Ndlovu.

This rather casual connection between my name and who I am has several important implications°. One of the most significant implications is the idea that the relationship between a word and the thing that it represents is arbitrary°. This means that the relationship between a word and what it represents is almost a matter of chance – it could have been called anything else and would still be the same thing.

A word is a sign: it conveys meaning and it can be interpreted. Whether this sign is made up of spoken noises or of written marks, the relationship between the sign and what it indicates is a human invention. Take, for example, a sign which we all know well: a red traffic light. There is no particular reason why a red light should mean 'stop' and a green light 'go'. They have these specific meanings only because a (large) group of people has chosen these signs to function in this way. We could change the signs and the meanings if we could persuade enough people to follow a new code.

Similarly, there is no magical connection between the word 'frog', for example, and the creature we call a frog. Another set of sounds or combinations of symbols could have been used just as well to indicate frog. Indeed, if you speak another language you will know this to be true. 'Frog' signifies frog because a linguistic° community (a group of speakers of that language) 'agrees' to attach the particular meaning to a particular sound pattern. In other words, meaning forms socially; it is not something that occurs automatically or naturally.

This arbitrary connection between a word and its meaning

NAMING: NOUNS AND PRONOUNS

Do you speak any language other than English?

If you do, does that language have the same kinds of pronouns as English does?

If the other language you speak does not have the same kinds of pronouns as English, how do the pronouns differ?

Pronouns are words which take the place of nouns, for example, I, you, he, they.

Nouns are words which name things.

Proper nouns name specific people, places or occasions, and they usually begin with a capital letter: Shakespeare, January, Johannesburg.

Common nouns refer to people, places and things in a more general way: kitchen, dog, car. Common nouns also refer to abstract qualities or states: humour, faithfulness, democracy.

raises an interesting question. If language is made socially, and if we as people establish our individual identities mainly through language – by saying 'I' or by giving ourselves specific names – to what extent are we 'made' by language and society? Is there something that can be called an essential, concrete self – an essence of individuality? Does each person have an 'inborn' identity that is not changed or shaped by their environment? Or is our identity, our position as individual people, something that is produced or made up by other people or by society?

These are difficult questions. They require much thought and even then they might be impossible to answer. Not reaching a definite answer, though, should not be seen as a weakness. You have made progress simply by not taking the idea of 'the self' for granted. In the next section we will look at some of the ways in which 'I' as a subject is unstable and uncertain.

. . . .

IN THIS SECTION we will explore ideas about our bodies and our minds and the roles they play in establishing a sense of self.

TWO

MIRRORS AND IDENTIKITS: HOW DO WE REPRESENT 'THE SELF'?

① Subjects as bodies

Let's begin by completing form P7-98 – an application for a passport for an imaginary country, Fantasia.

Department of State: Fantasia		P7-98
APPLICATION FOR A PASSPORT		

APPLICATION FOR: (mark which is applicable with an X)

Passport ☐1   Document for Travel Purposes ☐2

Emergency Passport ☐3   Child Passport/Endorsement ☐4

A. APPLICANT'S DETAILS

Surname ☐☐☐☐☐☐☐☐☐☐☐☐☐☐☐☐☐☐☐☐☐☐

Forenames in full ☐☐☐☐☐☐☐☐☐☐☐☐☐☐☐☐☐☐☐☐☐

Previous surname(s) ☐☐☐☐☐☐☐☐☐☐☐☐☐☐☐☐☐

Marital status: Single ☐ Married ☐ Widower ☐ Widow ☐

Divorced ☐ Sex: Male ☐ Female ☐

Y	Y	M	D

Date of birth ☐☐☐☐☐☐ ID Number ☐☐☐☐☐

Height (m) ☐☐ Mass(kg) ☐☐☐

Colour of hair (specify) ☐ Eye colour (specify) ☐

Place of birth ☐☐☐☐☐☐☐☐☐☐☐☐☐☐☐☐

Country of birth ☐☐☐☐☐☐☐☐☐☐☐☐☐☐☐☐

Address ☐☐☐☐☐☐☐☐☐☐☐☐☐☐☐☐☐☐☐☐

Home tel no. ☐☐☐☐☐☐☐☐☐☐☐☐☐☐☐☐☐

B. OFFICIAL USE ONLY, CERTIFICATION OF APPLICANT'S DETAILS

I, (Names in full) ....

designation (rank) ....

(a) all the necessary information has been obtained; and

(b) the photographs submitted with this application, are the photographs of
the person whose fingerprints, have been taken by me.

Y	Y	M	D

Signed .... Date ☐☐☐☐☐

Address ....

Photo of the applicant   Fingerprints of applicant

C. CITIZENSHIP

(a) Have you acquired citizenship of another country? YES NO If so, state
Country .... Means of obtaining .... Date ....

(b) Has a passport previously been issued to you? YES NO
When? ....

Passport/document number ☐☐☐☐☐☐☐☐☐☐☐☐☐☐☐☐

NOTE: Any passports or travel documents at present in the possession of the
applicant must be submitted with this application.

D. DECLARATION

I, ... declare that the information furnished above
is to the best of my knowledge and belief correct.

Date .... Place .... Signature ....

A passport, like an identity book, is a means by which we are identifiable. It establishes our individuality by separating us from other people. In a very real way it makes our claims to be individual people legal. One of the ways in which a passport does this is by noting our surname and our forenames. A passport also distinguishes between individual people in several other ways.

Most societies place emphasis on giving people fixed individual identities. We are often asked to prove that we are who we say we are. In many everyday situations we produce proofs of identity such as student cards, driver's licences or identity documents. Such documents connect the 'identity' we claim for ourselves to a unique set of physical characteristics. Producing such proof is usually not very difficult, because each of us has a combination of features that is unique to us. For example, I am male, thirty-nine years old, 1.86 metres tall, with brown eyes ... and so on. While millions of other people will be male, thirty-nine years old and 1.86 metres tall, only one will have that exact combination of features and characteristics that makes me identifiable as myself.

LIST FIVE WAYS in which a passport attempts to distinguish between individuals.

Why do you think society places such emphasis on legally verifiable identity? Why do you think that you cannot change your name without the consent of the state?

One of the reasons for linking a set of physical characteristics (usually represented by a photograph) to a name and then to a state-allocated code or identity number is to impose order on the mass of individuals that constitutes society. In certain respects then, identity is connected to control and to the exercise of power within society. Because we are individually identifiable in a legal sense we can be taxed, be educated to recognized levels, open bank accounts and enter into financial agreements, be married, be held accountable for our actions, and be allowed to vote. Without being able to distinguish between its citizens, a government could not do its job of governing, administering or providing.

● IN A WORLD where all the inhabitants looked exactly alike, would it be far more difficult to identify yourself? Or would we find others ways to do this?

Although for various reasons people often look cynically upon a government's attempts to impose 'order', the concept of identification becomes less questionable when the police and other legal authorities require it to prevent or solve crimes.

A CASE OF MISTAKEN IDENTITY?

In 1803 a New York City carpenter named Thomas Hoag, happily married and the father of a young daughter, suddenly disappeared. Two years later his sister-in-law heard his distinctive, lisping voice on the street behind her. Turning, she saw that the man behind her was indeed Hoag. She pointed him out to the authorities, and he was arrested for deserting his family. At his trial, eight people — including his landlord, his employer, and a close friend, identified him. He had a scar from when a horse had kicked him in the forehead and a recognizable wen (a benign tumour) on the back of his neck.

The defendant insisted that it was all a horrible coincidence, that he was one Joseph Parker, even going as far as to bring in eight witnesses of his own, including his wife of eight years to prove it. The judge couldn't decide.

Hoag's friend, with whom he used to exercise daily, remembered that Hoag had a large knife-scar on the bottom of his foot. The defendant was requested to take off his boots, which he gladly did. There was no scar. Parker went home to his wife. Hoag, as far as is known, was never found.

FROM: Michael Kurland, *How to Solve a Murder: The Forensic Handbook*. 1995. New York: Macmillan.

When a serious crime has been committed, police often draw up an Identikit to help them identify the culprit. Even 2 000 years ago the Roman empire was sending out letters describing missing criminals and runaway slaves. Scientific methods for identification are much more recent. In the 1880s Alphonse Bertillon, a records clerk with the Paris police, formulated a means of identifying criminals based on extremely detailed measurements of the body, the head and the limbs. These descriptive measurements have developed over the years. These days police use artists and computers to compile visual representations (Identikits) of suspects based on eyewitness descriptions. These Identikits are based on a form that is now more-or-less standard among most police forces. As you can see from the form reproduced below, this identification system is very detailed.

Try filling in the Identikit form using your own characteristics.

SUSPECT IDENTIFICATION FORM

Name .... Sex .... Colour ....

Nationality .... Occupation ....

Age .... Height .... Weight ....

Build   `large` `stout` `medium` `slim`

Complexion   `pale` `fair` `dark`

Hair   `long` `short` `thick` `thin` `bald` `partly bald` `straight` `curly` `wavy`

colour ....

Eyes   colour .... size .... shape ....

Eyebrows   `slanting` `up or down` `bushy or meeting` `arched` `wavy` `horizontal`

Texture   `strong` `thin` `short- or long-haired` `pencilled`

Nose   `small or large` `pug` `hooked` `straight` `flat`

Facial Hair   colour .... beard style ....

Chin   `small` `large` `square` `dimpled` `double` `flat`

Face   `long` `round` `square` `fat` `thin`

Neck   `long` `short` `thick` `thin` `folds in back of neck` `puffed neck`

`prominent Adam's apple`

Lips   `thick or thin` `puffy` `drooping lower or upturned upper`

Mouth   `large` `small` `drooping or upturned at corners` `open` `crooked`

`distorted during speech or laughter` `contorted`

Ears   `small` `large` `close to or projecting out from head` `pierced`

Distinctive Marks   `scars` `moles` `missing fingers or teeth` `gold teeth`

`tattoo marks` `lameness` `pockmarked` `flat feet` `nicotine fingers`

`freckles` `birthmarks`

Peculiarities   `twitching of features` `rapid or slow gait` `long or short steps`

`wearing of eyeglasses` `carrying a cane` `stuttering` `gruff voice`

`effeminate voice`

Jewellery   kind of .... where worn ....

Where likely to be found   `residence` `former residence` `places frequented`

`where employed` `residences of relatives, etc.`

Habits   `heavy drinker` `smoker` `drug addiction` `gambler` `clubs`

`frequenter of agencies` `discotheques` `cabarets` `sports events`

Suspect identification
form adapted from:
Michael Kurland,
*How to Solve a Murder:
The Forensic Hand-
book*. 1995. New York:
Macmillan

Of course, a difficulty for detectives tracking down criminals is that people change with time or are able to change their appearances deliberately, by undergoing plastic surgery or by wearing a disguise, for instance. Even the passport application form seems to acknowledge the difficulties of establishing identity on the basis of physical appearance alone. Read the following excerpts:

INSTRUCTIONS   P7-98
1   Husband, wife and children must complete separate Passport
    Application forms.
2   A Passport can only be issued to an individual who is in possession of a
    valid identification document.
3   A full set of finger prints is required from all applicants over the age of 16.
4   Two recent, clear full-face photographs (35 x 45 mm; head and shoulders
    only) of the applicant must accompany the application.
5   The certifying officer shall endorse the initials and surname of the
    applicant on the reverse side of the photographs.

CONDITIONS
1   Passports issued to adults are valid for 10 years from the date of issue.
2   Passports issued to children are valid for 5 years from the date of issue.
3   Only a child whose birth has been registered in terms of the Births
    Registration Act may be issued with a passport.

'People sometimes become puzzled by the notion of personal identity on being told that during any seven year period (or so) all the molecules in a human body are replaced by different ones'.

Sydney Shoemaker, *Self-Knowledge and Self-Identity*, pp. 5–6. 1963. Ithaca: Cornell University Press.

We need to ask ourselves whether changes in physical identity represent changes in 'the self'.

Since a sense of personal identity affects the interactions which make up our life experience, it is not surprising that literature and film often deal with the implications of human development and transformation. For instance, when Alice in Lewis Carroll's famous children's story *Alice's Adventures in Wonderland* falls down the rabbit hole and drinks from the bottle labelled 'Drink Me', strange things happen to her. Rapid changes in size and a succession of puzzling meetings with unusual creatures leave Alice confused. This confusion is made worse when she comes across a caterpillar sitting on a mushroom smoking a pipe called a hookah.

HE CATERPILLAR AND ALICE looked at each other for some time in silence: at last the Caterpillar took the hookah out of its mouth, and addressed her in a languid, sleepy voice.

'Who are *you*?' said the Caterpillar.

This was not an encouraging opening for a conversation. Alice replied, rather shyly, 'I – I hardly know sir, just at present – at least I know who I *was* when I got up this morning, but I think I must have changed several times since then.'

'What do you mean by that?' said the Caterpillar sternly. 'Explain yourself!'

'I can't explain *myself*, I'm afraid, sir,' said Alice, 'because I'm not myself, you see.'

'I don't see,' said the Caterpillar.

'I'm afraid I can't put it more clearly,' Alice replied very politely, 'for I can't understand it myself to begin with; and being so many different sizes in a day is very confusing.'

'It isn't,' said the Caterpillar.

'Well, perhaps you haven't found it so yet,' said Alice; 'but when you have to turn into a chrysalis – you will some day, you know – and then after that into a butterfly, I should think you'll feel it a little queer, won't you?'

'Not a bit,' said the Caterpillar.

'Well, perhaps your feelings may be different,' said Alice; 'all I know is, it would feel queer to *me*.'

'You!' said the Caterpillar contemptuously. 'Who are *you*?'

FROM: Lewis Carroll, *Alice's Adventures in Wonderland*, pp. 40–41. 1998. Oxford: Oxford University Press.

When the Caterpillar first asks Alice 'Who are *you*?' he simply wants her to identify herself. The second time, though, the question 'Who are *you*?' has an added barb. The way he asks it suggests that the Caterpillar has no respect for Alice and places no value on her understanding of change. The contemptuous tone tells us that the Caterpillar's question is a way of dismissing and devaluing Alice. For Alice, the recent rapid changes in her body have caused her to doubt her own identity. Alice is only the Alice she knows or remembers when she looks the way she is used to looking. The Caterpillar, on the other hand, denies that change should be a source of confusion. He knows that he will undergo a process of metamorphosis as an integral part of his life-cycle. Changing from a caterpillar into a chrysalis and then into a butterfly is normal for him.

● HOW MUCH can our bodies change, without us changing in some deep, inner way?

In Franz Kafka's short novel *The Metamorphosis* (1916) a young man wakes up one morning to find himself transformed into a giant beetle-like insect. The narrator stresses that this is not a dream and the story explores how this change wreaks havoc on the young man's identity. Here is the first paragraph of the story. Read it imagining that this has happened to you.

HEN GREGOR SAMSA woke up one morning from unsettling dreams, he found himself changed in his bed into a monstrous vermin. He was lying on his back as hard as armor plate, and when he lifted his head a little, he saw his vaulted brown belly, sectioned by arch-shaped ribs, to whose dome the cover, about to slide off completely, could barely cling. His many legs, pitifully thin compared with the size of the rest of him, were waving helplessly before his eyes.

FROM: Franz Kafka, *The Metamorphosis*.
1981. New York: Bantam.

Samsa knows who he is even though his body is unrecognizable. Other people, however, no longer relate to him in the same way as they did before. His experience is used as a symbol for human alienation in the modern age.

1
Myles with bottle and hammer in overalls at age three.

One level at which change occurs in all human beings is in the body. All humans experience physical change, but very few feel that these changes have left them unrecognizable. And yet, look at these two versions of me.

AUTOBIOGRAPHY

- Can I say that 'the self' represented in the first photograph is 'the self' represented in the second?
- Apart from physical changes, which other changes might have occurred that might not be visible in the second photograph?
- Moreover, can I say that 'the self' in the earlier photograph inevitably and naturally led to 'the self' in the later photograph?
- If I had grown up under different circumstances, would I have been exactly the same person?

2
Myles aged thirty-nine years and five months.

TIME OFF

TO THINK ABOUT
CHANGES IN YOURSELF

If you have a photograph of yourself taken ten or twenty years ago, look at it and then look into the mirror.

- How have you changed?
- What caused these changes?
- Have you changed psychologically as well as physically?
  If so, describe the changes that have occurred.
- Has any part of you remained constant? If so, which part? Why?
- Where do you think the most change in the identity of a person occurs over the years?

2 Internal profiles

In the light of what you have read about personal change and development, read the following poem. 'The Road Not Taken' raises ideas that are relevant to our exploration of 'the self' as it looks at the question of choice and consequences. In life any choice involves a whole range of possible future experiences. But a decision leading one way excludes another set of possible experiences.

ROBERT FROST
(1874–1963)
wrote many poems
about life in rural
America, but
because we do not
know whether a
particular piece is
autobiographical
or not we refer to
the 'I' in the poem
as 'the speaker'.

THE ROAD NOT TAKEN
Robert Frost

Two roads diverged in a yellow wood,
And sorry I could not travel both
And be one traveller, long I stood
And looked down one as far as I could
To where it bent in the undergrowth;

Then took the other, as just as fair,
And having perhaps the better claim,
Because it was grassy and wanted wear;
Though as for that, the passing there
Had worn them really about the same,

And both that morning equally lay
In leaves no step had trodden black.
Oh, I kept the first for another day!
Yet knowing how way leads on to way,
I doubted if I should ever come back.

I shall be telling this with a sigh
Somewhere ages and ages hence:
Two roads diverged in a wood, and I -
I took the one less travelled by,
And that has made all the difference.

FROM: *The Poetry of Robert Frost,*
Henry Holt & Company.

In the poem the speaker makes the point that she or he 'could not travel both [roads]/ And be one traveller'. This idea illustrates the way in which identity seems to depend on experience. A single

AUTOBIOGRAPHY

'traveller' cannot go in two directions at the same time, in the same way that we cannot live two completely different kinds of lives at the same time. To explore this idea in more detail, read the following passage. The passage is an extract° from a conversation between two people. In the conversation, one person is interviewing the other about his life and experiences.

LARRY (THE INTERVIEWER): We have spoken about so much today, your fame, your achievements, your career, your goals, but I feel there is a side of you I haven't seen yet. Your childhood – your origins ... where do you come from?

J. B.: Well actually, Larry, this is a side of me I don't really talk about much. You'll see why, I suppose. The thing is, where I come from isn't a simple matter. In 1968 a child was born in one of the largest hospitals in New York City. At birth the child (a boy, average weight, healthy) was given a name; he was 'Carlos'. His parents hadn't lived in the city for long – actually, Larry, they were just kids. In fact, Larry, they had only come to America about a year before he was born. They were young, poor and had no jobs – and they spoke no English, which made it hard to find good jobs. The mother's family was very ashamed of her and persuaded her that she would never be able to provide for her baby. They were already a large family and were living in a two-room apartment with taps that gave out no water and windows that let the cold, winter air blow through the room; what would they do with a tiny new baby?

And so, Larry, what happens? She gives him up for adoption. One month into the infant boy's life, he is handed over to his new family. The couple who have taken him are middle-class, English-speaking and unable to have children themselves. Together the family travel to a distant city in the mid-West and a new house. They buy a pram, a crib, clothes, diapers and toys – they paint clouds and rainbows on the bedroom walls. The child is named John.

I am John.

I am Carlos.

So when I look at myself in a mirror, Larry, who do I see? Do I see the child left in an orphanage, or do I see the consequences of the life I have led? What might I be now if I had stayed Carlos? These are questions I still cannot answer, over thirty years later....

If I apply the ideas raised by this piece of autobiography to my own circumstances, then they also suggest that who I am today is not simply a matter of who I was when I was born. My background, the home in which I grew up, my education and the experiences I have had all contribute to my identity now. Given a different set of circumstances, I may have been a very different person. This, in turn, suggests that my identity – my sense of 'self' – is not simply physical. As a 'self' I also define myself inwardly in terms of personality, emotions and achievements. While I might not be as uncertain about who I am as Alice is in *Alice's Adventures in Wonderland*, I do not think of identity as entirely certain or fixed.

PERSONALITY

Although experts differ in their definition and understanding of personality, the term is generally used to describe deeply ingrained, relatively persistent patterns of thought, feeling and behaviour in a person. Like physical characteristics, personality also refers to what is unique about a particular person. In other words, characteristics (also known as traits) or combinations of characteristics (such as kindness, intelligence, aggressiveness, competitiveness or reliability) are applied to individuals to distinguish them from other people. Used like this, the term personality covers many aspects of individuality.

The most obvious aspects are what is sometimes called 'temperament' – a person's typical emotional and behavioural reactions. Thus we might speak of someone as 'shy', 'outgoing' or 'quick-tempered' to describe the ways they behave or the ways others perceive them. Some aspects of personality are less obvious because they are not necessarily visible to casual observers. These aspects of personality include abilities, beliefs, attitudes, values and motives. Intelligence, religious faith and personal attitudes concerning appropriate or inappropriate behaviour fall into this category°. Unlike physical characteristics which are readily visible, personality is something that can be hidden or concealed, inwardly. What people observe in others, then, are outward expressions of personality in the form of particular types of behaviour. We cannot always see the reasons why a person acts or reacts in a certain way. Yet, together with naming and physical description, personality is a means of categorizing and differ-entiating people.

Look at the identikit form again. Notice that it blurs the distinction between physical characteristics and behaviour. Here are the last four categories from the Suspect Identification Form:

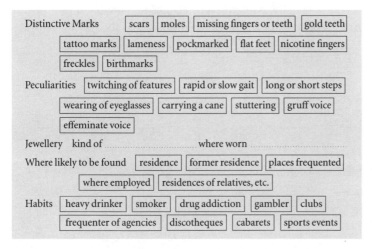

Distinctive Marks — scars — moles — missing fingers or teeth — gold teeth — tattoo marks — lameness — pockmarked — flat feet — nicotine fingers — freckles — birthmarks

Peculiarities — twitching of features — rapid or slow gait — long or short steps — wearing of eyeglasses — carrying a cane — stuttering — gruff voice — effeminate voice

Jewellery   kind of .... where worn ....

Where likely to be found — residence — former residence — places frequented — where employed — residences of relatives, etc.

Habits — heavy drinker — smoker — drug addiction — gambler — clubs — frequenter of agencies — discotheques — cabarets — sports events

✪ Which items in these categories do you think are relevant to personality?
✪ Is it possible to separate personality from a person's physical being?

The extent to which our personalities are determined by our genetic inheritance has been the subject° of much controversy and research. Many would argue we are genetically predisposed to certain behavioural patterns, but that social, cultural and environmental influences also have a significant effect on personality. Schooling, for instance, influences a person's ability to perform certain tasks. Education also

Police squads investigating serial murder cases employ specialist psychologists to draw up psychological and social profiles of the killer or killers. By studying clues left at crime scenes and especially patterns of behaviour that emerge from each incident, these experts are able to draw up detailed profiles that assist in identifying suspects.

shapes people's attitudes to events and issues. Our concern, though, is not with the origins of personality. We are interested in how we think of ourselves as personalities, and with the ways we show or express our personalities to other people in action and writing.

PUTTING OURSELVES TO THE TEST .... FOR FUN!

THIS QUIZ is not a serious, psychological evaluation. It is intended to be an enjoyable way for you to explore your personality.

What follows is a short personality test similar to those that often appear in magazines. We have included it as an opportunity for you to think about some of the ways in which personal identity is understood and represented. Various statements appear in the first column. In the next columns, tick the boxes (Always, Usually, Sometimes or Never) that you think apply to you.

		Always	Usually	Sometimes	Never
1	I enjoy spending time with friends.	☐	☐	☐	☐
2	I am very talkative and full of energy.	☐	☐	☐	☐
3	I enjoy talking about myself.	☐	☐	☐	☐
4	I think of myself as a relaxed person.	☐	☐	☐	☐
5	I encourage other people to talk about themselves.	☐	☐	☐	☐
6	I care about other people's feelings.	☐	☐	☐	☐
7	I often criticize and judge other people.	☐	☐	☐	☐
8	I worry about things.	☐	☐	☐	☐
9	I am calm in difficult situations.	☐	☐	☐	☐
10	I enjoy working with other people as part of a group.	☐	☐	☐	☐
11	I am quiet in a group and do not like to start a conversation.	☐	☐	☐	☐
12	Other people think that I am a nervous person.	☐	☐	☐	☐
13	Other people think I am fun to be with.	☐	☐	☐	☐
14	I treat people rudely, especially if I don't like them.	☐	☐	☐	☐
15	I am tolerant of other people's points of view.	☐	☐	☐	☐
16	It is important to me that I should be well liked.	☐	☐	☐	☐
17	It is important to me that my appearance should make a good impression on others.	☐	☐	☐	☐
18	I expect other people to agree with me and follow my advice.	☐	☐	☐	☐
19	I am happy to help someone even if it causes me difficulty.	☐	☐	☐	☐
20	I am honest with people even if I feel my opinions might be hurtful to them.	☐	☐	☐	☐

What do you think your answers to this quiz reveal about your personality?

Here are descriptions of two very different personality types. Your answers to the first five questions above could place you closer to one category or the other. Where do you belong?

If you answered 'Never' to questions 1 to 5 you are an introvert:	**If you answered 'Always' to questions 1 to 5 you are an extrovert:**
You love spending time on your own. You find other people's company demanding and exhausting. You do not like socializing. You are inward-looking. Your idea of fun is being alone at home with a book for company. You really don't like parties and working in groups. Other people see you as being quiet, shy or reserved.	You are energized by spending time with other people. You love socializing, talking and being around others. You enjoy parties and social situations. You are talkative and need to communicate with the world around you. Your worst nightmare is being forced to spend much time alone. Your life is directed outwards: towards things and people around you.

✪ Would you say that either of these types accurately describes your personality?

✪ Write down the characteristics that you think would be a more truthful representation of yourself.

Generally, this kind of personality quiz works on a series of assumptions° about people and how they view themselves. Most tests are not entirely accurate. At best, they can be used as starting points for thinking about aspects of your personality. One of the limitations of a test like this is that it uses stereotypes°. A stereotype is an unfairly fixed and standardized version of a person or thing. It is not an accurate representation. Stereotypes emphasize particular characteristics and distort the complex reality of what is being described. They are often associated with prejudice° and can be hurtful and offensive. We will explore stereotypes and prejudice in more detail later in this book. For the moment, we will focus on one aspect of stereotypes: the idea that they are fixed.

There are two problems with the concept of fixed personality

● THINK of the way that you behave in different situations; for instance, when you are by yourself, when you are with close friends and when you are in the company of strangers. Do you feel and behave in exactly the same way in all these situations?

● DO YOU have a
personality that
you show in public,
for instance at work
or in formal social
situations, that is
different from the
way that you
behave in private?
● TO WHAT extent
can you control or
adapt your respon-
ses according to the
situation in which
you find yourself?

types. The first is that a fixed personality type allows no room for development and change. If one assumes that personalities are fixed from birth, then the personality of the child will become the personality of the adult. A fixed personality would not develop or alter with experience. The second problem is that the idea of a fixed personality does not take into account that people can often control what parts of their personality they choose to reveal in different circumstances.

If people do have some degree of control over their personality and how they show it, who and what we are is not just formed socially; our identity is also made by us, deliberately, by our own choice. (Of course, what we consider deliberate behaviour may itself be deeply socialized.) Finally, changes in the personality that we project suggest that who we are, to some extent, depends on how we present ourselves and how our presentations are viewed by other people. The next section explores this point in more detail.

MEETING MADIBA

The name 'Nelson Mandela' is known around the world. Whether they support his politics or not, many people seem to feel that they know all about this prisoner who became president. People have an idea of who he is, but how much is known of the man, Nelson Mandela? Can we distinguish between his personal and his political identities? How has Mandela made himself into the figure that is so familiar? In this section, we will examine some of these questions with the help of Nelson Mandela's auto-biography, *Long Walk to Freedom*, which was published in 1994.

Person and politician

So what is the connection between Nelson Rolihlahla Mandela's public personality and how we view him personally?
✪ Write down five words that you think best describe how most people see Nelson Mandela.

❂ Now write down five words which describe how you personally see him.

❂ Do these two sets of words have anything in common? For instance, do they have positive or negative connotations?° Do they deal with Mandela's career as a politician or with his private life?

If I had to guess what sort of words you have used to describe Nelson Mandela, I would guess that they are associated with his role as a leader and politician. Depending on your political beliefs, these words might be favourable or unfavourable.

To me, the name 'Nelson Mandela' suggests the long struggle against racial oppression, great personal sacrifice and suffering for the cause of justice, and the dignity of the prisoner–president who feels no hatred for his former captors. Other people might use derogatory terms, like 'terrorist', for instance, to describe him. I am almost certain that the words that you have chosen have little to do with Nelson Mandela's physical features or his private thoughts and desires. Our sense of the person, Nelson Mandela, is determined by those aspects of his identity that we choose to focus on. His identity and what that identity means for us are things that we create in our own minds from the messages we get about him in the media, from what other people tell us, and from what we decide to believe.

At the same time, Nelson Mandela is an active maker of his own identity. What he says and does and what he chooses to reveal about himself have an enormous impact on our perceptions of his identity. How Nelson Mandela selects information about himself to share is particularly clear from his autobiography, which, by definition, is a public statement of his private person.

WHAT'S IN A NAME?

MADIBA:
Nelson Mandela's clan name, used as a mark of respect and affection.

NELSON:
an English name given to Mandela on his first day at school by his teacher Miss Mdingane. He was seven years old.

ROLIHLAHLA:
the Xhosa name given to Mandela at birth by his father. Literally, it means 'pulling the branch of a tree', but its colloquial meaning is 'troublemaker'.

MANDELA:
his family name

Look at the contents page of *Long Walk to Freedom*. The table of contents of a book provides valuable information about what we can expect as we read on.

CONTENTS

- ✪ WHICH CHAPTERS do you think deal with Mandela's personal life?
- ✪ WHICH CHAPTERS seem to deal with his political activities and experiences?
- ✪ WHAT ASPECTS of his life do you think Mandela's autobiography will choose to emphasize?
- ✪ WHY DO YOU think the autobiography emphasizes the things it does?
- ✪ PLAN the contents page of your own autobiography. What would each of your chapters be called?

The following excerpt from Nelson Mandela's life story is set in the 1940s when he is twenty-three years old. To escape a marriage arranged for him by his guardian, the regent of Thembuland, Mandela flees to Johannesburg, where, after working briefly as a mine policeman, he secures a position as a clerk with a law firm – Witkin, Sildelsky and Eidelmann – at a salary of £2 per week. Although this sum is hardly enough to live on, the young Mandela finds accommodation in the backyard room of a house belonging to a Mr Xhoma in Alexandra.

QUICK QUIZ: how well do you know Nelson Mandela?
- Where was he born?
- When was he born?
- Where did he go to high school?
- What was his first job?
- On what day was he released after twenty-seven years in prison?

HE XHOMA FAMILY had five daughters, each of them lovely, but the loveliest of all was named Didi. Didi was about my age and spent most of the week working as a domestic worker in a white suburb of Johannesburg. When I first moved to the house, I saw her only seldom and fleetingly. But later, when I made her acquaintance properly, I also fell in love with her. But Didi barely took any notice of me, and what she did notice was the fact that I owned only one patched-up suit and a single shirt, and that I did not present a figure much different from a tramp.

Every weekend Didi returned to Alexandra. She was brought home by a young man whom I assumed was her boyfriend, a flashy, well-to-do fellow who had a car, something that was most unusual. He wore expensive, double-breasted American suits and wide-brimmed hats, and paid a great deal of attention to his appearance. He must have been a gangster of some sort, but I cannot be sure. He would stand outside in the yard and put his hands in his waistcoat and look altogether superior. He greeted me politely, but I could see that he did not regard me as much competition.

I yearned to tell Didi I loved her, but I was afraid that my advances would be unwanted. I was hardly a Don Juan. Awkward and hesitant around girls, I did not know or understand the romantic games that others seemed to play effortlessly. On weekends, Didi's mother would sometimes ask her to bring out a plate of food to me. Didi would arrive on my doorstep with the plate and I could tell that she simply wanted to perform her errand as quickly as possible, but I would do my best to delay her. I would query her opinion on things, all sorts of questions. 'Now, what standard did you attain in school?' I would say. Standard five, she replied. 'Why did you leave?' I asked. She was bored, she replied. 'Ah, well, you must go back to school,' I said. 'You are about the same age as I am,' I continued, 'and there is nothing wrong with returning to school at this age. Otherwise you will regret it when you are old. You must think seriously about your future. It is nice for you now because you are young and beautiful and have many admirers, but you need to have an independent profession.'

I realize that these are not the most romantic words that have ever been uttered by a young man to a young woman with whom he was in love, but I did not know what else to talk to her about. She listened seriously, but I could tell that she was not interested in me, that in fact she felt a bit superior to me.

I wanted to propose to her but I was unwilling to do so unless I was certain she would say yes. Although I loved her, I did not want to give her the satisfaction of rejecting me. I kept up my pursuit of her, but I was timid and hesitant. In love, unlike politics, caution is not usually a virtue. I was neither confident enough to think that I might succeed nor secure enough to bear the sense of failure if I did not.

I stayed at that house for about a year, and in the end, I uttered nothing about my feelings.

Nelson Mandela, *Long Walk to Freedom*,
pp. 69–71. 1994. Boston: Little, Brown.

✪ Does this extract surprise you in any way? If it does, can you think of the reason why you find it surprising? Was its subject matter unexpected?

✪ Have you ever been in a situation similar to the one described in the passage? If you have, how did you react? Were you able to show your feelings?

✪ What does his inability to tell Didi of his love reveal about Mandela's personality at the time?

✪ What do his conversations with Didi reveal of Mandela's values?

✪ Look up the following words in a dictionary. Write down their definitions and tick the words you would use to describe Mandela at this time.

sophisticated ☐	intelligent ☐	naïve ☐
insecure ☐	articulate ☐	proud ☐
experienced ☐	confident ☐	awkward ☐
romantic ☐	foolish ☐	suave ☐
gregarious ☐	principled ☐	

How do you think Nelson Mandela, as an elderly man, would feel about this youthful infatuation?

We meet Madiba again almost twenty years later. He is no longer a shy, love-struck youth. While living in Johannesburg, studying through UNISA and then at Wits, and mixing with politically aware South Africans of all races, Mandela joined the African National Congress Youth League as a founder-member in 1944. His organizational skills and his commitment to the ideal of black liberation saw a rapid growth in his influence; ultimately it also brought him unwanted attention from the security police.

THE AFRICAN NATIONAL CONGRESS (ANC) was founded in 1912 as a non-violent civil-rights organization that worked to promote the interests of black South Africans. For the first fifty years of its existence, the organization stressed constitutional means to achieve change, using delegations, petitions, passive resistance, strikes and peaceful protest. The membership of the ANC increased rapidly after the National Party came to power in 1948 and began to implement its policy of rigid, legislated racial segregation. In 1955 the ANC adopted the Freedom Charter, which stated (among other things) that 'South Africa belongs to all who live in it, black and white'. As the white minority government implemented its policies with increasingly oppressive force, the ANC began to recognize the futility of non-violent protest, and formed a military wing, Umkhonto we Sizwe in 1961, with the aim of beginning a sabotage campaign. The subsequent imprisonment of ANC leaders did little to quell black resistance, and in 1990 the Nationalist government finally abandoned apartheid. Negotiations during the early 1990s led to South Africa's first non-racial, democratic election in April 1994, which the ANC won by a large majority.

30 July 1952
Arrested (with twenty-one other leaders) and charged under the Suppression of Communism Act.

2 December 1952
Sentenced to nine months imprisonment with hard labour, suspended for two years.

December 1952
Banned (with fifty-two other leaders) for six months. Prohibited from attending meetings.

EIGHT GUILTY IN RIVONIA TRIAL

Seven on all four charges and one on one coun

BERNSTEIN FREE REARRESTED

PRETORIA, Thurs

SEVEN of the nine accused in the Rivonia sabotage found guilty on all four counts in the Supreme Pretoria, to-day.

MRS. BERNSTEIN AND DAUGHTER IN TEARS

Natives shout and sin

March 1960
Arrested and imprisoned without trial (while out on bail during the treason trial) under State of Emergency regulations. Held for five months.

3 September 1953
Receives banning order for two years under Suppression of Communism Act. Required by law to resign from the ANC. Restricted to the Johannesburg District. Prohibited from attending meetings or gatherings.

December 1956
Arrested with 155 other leaders. Charged with high treason. Acquitted in March 1961 after a trial lasting four years.

March 1956
Banned for five years. Restricted to the Johannesburg District. Prohibited from attending meetings or gatherings.

HINTS AND STRATEGIES FOR READING

Sometimes it is useful, when faced with reading something for academic purposes, to *survey* it before reading it in detail. In other words, you read to gain a general impression° of the writer's argument before examining the ideas in detail. There are two useful strategies° for getting a general impression.

Firstly, you can *skim*. When you skim you read very quickly, deliberately leaving out parts of the text to get the main ideas. It is useful to:

✪ look at the title and any subheadings;

✪ look at any captions or illustrations;

✪ look at words written in bold, italics or capitals;

✪ quickly read the first and last paragraphs of the text, since writers often summarize their ideas in these paragraphs; and

✪ quickly read the first sentence of each paragraph, as this will often contain the main idea of the paragraph.

Secondly, you can *scan*. When you scan a text, you are reading to find a particular idea or piece of information. You usually let your eyes pass quickly over the page looking for specific information without reading the whole text.

After surveying the article, the next step is to read it carefully and thoughtfully. In other words, read it in detail. This is also sometimes called the *study-read* phase. There are many ways of reading a text carefully. One very useful strategy is, if you come across words you do not understand, to re-read the sentence in which the word appears and then re-read the surrounding sentences. If you cannot guess the meaning in this way, look up the word in a dictionary (or in the book's glossary if there is one). If you use a dictionary, make sure that you select a meaning that fits the context°. Practise these skills on the extracts from *Long Walk to Freedom*.

ADAPTED FROM:
START: *Strategies for Academic Reading and Thinking.* 1996.
Pietermaritzburg:
Shuter & Shooter.

The National Party government would stop at nothing in their quest to crush all black opposition to apartheid. The ANC, therefore, decided to operate underground as a covert political organization. Mandela was an active planner and organizer, secretly travelling around the country and leaving South Africa illegally to secure international support for the ANC. During this time he became a newspaper celebrity for his ability to evade arrest. His luck ran out in August 1962 though, when he was caught by the police near Howick in what is today KwaZulu-Natal. This time he was sentenced to five years in prison (three for inciting workers to strike and two for leaving the country without a valid passport), without possibility of parole. He would not taste freedom for another twenty-seven years.

A police raid on Liliesleaf Farm – an ANC safe house in Rivonia near Johannesburg – in July 1963 unearthed detailed documentation regarding Operation Mayibuye, which was a plan for guerrilla warfare to be conducted by Umkhonto we Sizwe, the ANC's military wing. As a key member of the High Command Mandela found himself in court again. The charge was high treason.

The following extract is from Nelson Mandela's speech to the court at what became known as the Rivonia Treason Trial.

ROSE AND FACED THE COURTROOM AND READ SLOWLY.

I am the first accused.

I hold a Bachelor's degree in Arts, and practised as an attorney in Johannesburg for a number of years in partnership with Mr Oliver Tambo. I am a convicted prisoner, serving five years for leaving the country without a permit and for inciting people to go on strike at the end of May 1961.

I admit immediately that I was one of the persons who helped to form Umkhonto we Sizwe and that I played a prominent role in its affairs until I was arrested in August 1962.

At the outset, I want to say that the suggestion

made by the state in its opening that the struggle in South Africa is under the influence of foreigners or Communists is wholly incorrect. I have done whatever I did, both as an individual and as a leader of my people, because of my experience in South Africa, and my own proudly felt African background, and not because of what any outsider might have said.

In my youth in the Transkei, I listened to the elders of my tribe telling stories of the old days. Amongst the tales they related to me were those of wars fought by our ancestors in defence of the fatherland. The names of Dingane and Bambatha, Hintsa and Makanna, Squngthi and Dalasile, Moshoeshoe and Sekhukhuni were praised as the pride and glory of the entire African nation. I hoped then that life might offer me the opportunity to serve my people and make my own humble contribution to their freedom struggle. This is what has motivated me in all that I have done in relation to the charges made against me in this case.

Having said this, I must deal immediately and at some length with the question of violence. Some of the things so far told the court are true and some are untrue. I do not, however, deny that I planned sabotage. I did not plan it in a spirit of recklessness nor because I have any love of violence. I planned it as a result of a calm and sober assessment of the political situation that had arisen after many years of tyranny, exploitation, and oppression of my people by whites.

I wanted to impress upon the court that we had not acted irresponsibly or without thought to the ramifications of taking up violent action. I laid particular emphasis on our resolve to cause no harm to human life.

We of the ANC have always stood for a non-racial democracy, and we shrank from any action which might drive the races further apart than they already were. But the hard facts were that fifty years of non-violence had brought the African people nothing but more repressive legislation, and fewer and fewer rights. It may not be easy for this court to understand, but it is a fact that for a long time the people had been talking of violence – of the day when they would fight the white man and win back their country, and we, the leaders of the ANC, had nevertheless always prevailed upon them to avoid violence and to use peaceful methods. While some of us discussed this in May and June of 1961, it could not be denied that our policy to achieve a non-racial state by non-violence had achieved nothing, and that our followers were beginning to lose confidence in this policy and were developing disturbing ideas of terrorism....

Umkhonto was formed in November 1961. When we took this decision, and subsequently formulated our plans, the ANC heritage of non-violence and racial harmony was very much with us. We felt that the country was drifting towards a civil war in which blacks and whites would fight each other. We viewed the situation with alarm. Civil war would mean the destruction of what the ANC stood for; with civil war racial peace would be more difficult than ever to achieve. We already have examples in South African history of the results of war. It has taken more than fifty years for the scars of the South African [Anglo-Boer] War to disappear. How much longer would it take to eradicate the scars of interracial civil war, which could not be fought without a great loss of life on both sides?

Sabotage, I said, offered the best hope for future race relations. The reaction of the white rulers to our first efforts were swift and brutal: sabotage was declared to be a crime punishable by death. We did not want civil war, I said, but we needed to be prepared for it.

Experience convinced us that rebellion would offer the government limitless opportunities for the indiscriminate slaughter of our people. But it was precisely because the soil of South Africa is already drenched with the blood of innocent Africans that we felt it our duty to make preparations as a long-term undertaking to use force in order to defend ourselves against force. If war were inevitable, we wanted the fight to be conducted on terms most favourable to our people. The fight which held out prospects best for us and the least risk of life to both sides was guerrilla warfare. We decided, therefore, in our preparations for the future, to make provision for the possibility of guerrilla warfare. [...]

I explained that at this stage in our discussions I left the country to attend the PAFMECSA conference and undergo military training. I said that I underwent training because if there was to be a guerrilla war, I wanted to be able to stand and fight beside my own people. Even so, I believed that the possibilities of sabotage were far from exhausted and should be pursued with vigour.

I told the court of the dividing line between the ANC and MK, and how we made good-faith attempts to keep the two separate. This was our policy, but in practice, it was not so simple. Because of bannings and imprisonment, people often had to work in both organizations. Though this might have sometimes blurred the distinction, it did not abolish it. I disputed the allegations of the state that the aims and objects of the ANC and the Communist Party were one and the same. [...]

I told the court that I was not a Communist and had always regarded myself as an African patriot. I did not deny that I was attracted by the idea of a classless society, or that I had been influenced by Marxist thought. This was true of many leaders of the newly independent states of Africa, who accepted the need for some form of socialism to enable their people to catch up with the advanced countries of the West.

From my reading of Marxist literature and from conversations with Marxists, I have gained the impression that Communists regard the parliamentary system of the West as undemocratic and reactionary. But, on the contrary, I am an admirer of such a system.

The Magna Carta, the Petition of Rights and the Bill of Rights are documents which are held in veneration by democrats throughout the world. I have great respect for British political institutions, and for the country's system of justice. I regard the British Parliament as the most democratic institution in the world, and the independence and impartiality of its judiciary never fail to arouse my admiration. The American Congress, the country's doctrine of separation of powers, as well as the independence of its judiciary, arouse in me similar sentiments.

I detailed the terrible disparities between black and white life in South Africa. In education, health, income, every aspect of life, blacks were barely at a subsistence level while whites had the highest standards in the world – and aimed to keep it that way. Whites, I said, often claimed that Africans in South Africa were better off than Africans in the rest of the continent. Our complaint, I said, was not that we were poor by comparison with the people in the rest of Africa, but that we were poor by comparison with the whites in our country, and that we were prevented by legislation from righting that imbalance.

The lack of human dignity experienced by Africans is the direct result of the policy of white supremacy. White supremacy implies black inferiority. Legislation designed to preserve white supremacy entrenches this notion. Menial tasks in South Africa are invariably performed by Africans. When anything has to be carried or cleaned the white man looks around for an African to do it for him, whether the African is employed by him or not. ...

Poverty and the breakdown of family life have secondary effects. Children wander about the streets of the townships because they have no schools to go to, or no money to enable them to go to school, or no parents at home to see that they go to school, because both parents (if there be two) have to work to keep the family alive. This leads to a breakdown in moral standards, to an alarming rise in illegitimacy and to growing violence which erupts, not only politically, but everywhere. ...

Africans want a just share in the whole of South Africa; they want security and a stake in society. Above all, we want equal political rights, because without them our disabilities will be permanent. I know this sounds revolutionary to the white in this country, because the majority of voters will be Africans. This makes the white man fear democracy. ...

This then is what the ANC is fighting for. Their struggle is a truly national one. It is a struggle of the African people, inspired by their own suffering and their own experience. It is a struggle for the right to live.

I had been reading my speech, and at this point I placed my papers on the defence table, and turned to face the judge. The courtroom became extremely quiet. I did not take my eyes off Justice de Wet as I spoke from memory the final words.

During my lifetime, I have dedicated myself to this struggle of the African people. I have fought against white domination, and I have fought against black domination. I have cherished the ideal of a democratic and free society in which all persons live together in harmony and with equal opportunities. It is an ideal which I hope to live for and to achieve. But if needs be, it is an ideal for which I am prepared to die.

The silence in the courtroom was now complete. At the end of the address, I simply sat down. I did not turn and face the gallery, thought I felt all their eyes on me. The silence seemed to stretch for many minutes. But in fact it lasted probably no more than thirty seconds, and then from the gallery I heard what sounded like a great sigh, a deep, collective 'ummmm', followed by the cries of women.

Nelson Mandela, *Long Walk to Freedom*, pp. 317–322. 1994. Boston: Little, Brown.

✪ How do you feel after reading this extract?

✪ Which of the two extracts, this one or the one describing his unspoken love for Didi, do you associate most strongly with Nelson Mandela?

✪ Look at the list of words that you used to describe Mandela as a young man. Which of these words would you use to describe his courtroom personality and performance?
Are there other words that you would add?

✪ Make a list of the issues that Nelson Mandela deals with in the Rivonia speech. What do these issues have in common?

✪ What do the following words reveal about Nelson Mandela's personality? 'I do not, however, deny that I planned sabotage. I did not plan it in a spirit of recklessness nor because I have any love of violence. I planned it as a result of a calm and sober assessment of the political situation that had arisen after many years of tyranny, exploitation, and oppression of my people by whites.'

✪ Does Mandela's Rivonia Treason Trial speech tell us anything about him as a person, or is it purely political?

The Rivonia Treason Trial speech is clearly Nelson Mandela's political manifesto, both personally and as a representative of the African National Congress. In explaining his actions, he is explaining the actions of his organization too. Throughout the speech and throughout *Long Walk to Freedom*, Mandela the person is almost inseparable from the cause that has shaped his life.

Of course, his speech also reveals much about the man's inner nature. His idealism, his commitment to democracy, his sense of human dignity, his insistence on equality and his opposition to all forms of injustice are obvious. Moreover, given the fact that he was facing the possibility of being sentenced to death, the Rivonia speech is a remarkable statement of Mandela's personal courage and of his unselfish willingness to place the good of a wider community of others before his own interests. We are left with the feeling that Mandela is a man who speaks honestly and directly.

His honesty and directness, however, do not imply that Mandela's speech to the court was not carefully planned and structured. Throughout the speech and throughout Mandela's autobiographical account of the speech we have evidence that the words Mandela uses are carefully selected and placed in order to achieve the greatest possible effect. These are public statements uttered before a courtroom, and, since the press would publish the speech throughout the world, before a huge international audience°. It stands to reason that Mandela would want to make the best of his opportunity to outline his case. Thus, although we never doubt the sincerity of his statements, we are aware that these statements are formulated and delivered in a manner that will present a powerful and favourable image of Mandela and the ANC. This is particularly clear in the final paragraphs of the extract from the Rivonia Treason Trial speech. Notice how Mandela stops reading his speech and addresses the judge directly from memory.

✪ Why does Mandela address the judge directly towards the end of the speech? What effect does this direct, spoken (rather than read) statement have?

✪ How does Mandela characterize himself in the final words of his speech?

✪ What does the reaction of the people in the courtroom suggest about the impact of the speech on its listeners?

 Unspoken texts

The idea of writing an autobiography was first suggested to Mandela in 1975 while he was still a prisoner on Robben Island.

 NE DAY, KATHY [Ahmed Kathrada], Walter [Sisulu] and I were talking in the courtyard when they suggested that I ought to write my memoirs. Kathy noted that the perfect time for such a book to be published would be on my sixtieth birthday. Walter said that such a story, if told truly and fairly, would serve to remind people of what we had fought and were still fighting for. He added that it could become a source of inspiration for young freedom fighters. The idea appealed to me, and during subsequent discussion, I agreed to go ahead. [...]

We created an assembly line to process the manuscript. Each day I passed on what I wrote to Kathy, who reviewed the manuscript, and then read it to Walter. Kathy then wrote their comments in the margins. Walter and Kathy have never hesitated to criticize me, and I took their suggestions to heart, often incorporating their changes. This marked-up manuscript was then given to Laloo Chiba, who spent the next night transferring my writing to his own almost microscopic shorthand, reducing ten pages of foolscap to a single small piece of paper. It would be Mac's [Maharaj] job to smuggle the manuscript to the outside world.

[...] I wrote rapidly, completing a draft in four months. I did not hesitate over choosing a word or phrase. I covered the period from my birth through the Rivonia Trial, and ended with some notes about Robben Island.

I relived my experiences as I wrote about them. Those nights, as I wrote in silence, I could once again experience the sights and sounds of my youth in Qunu and Mqhekezwini; the excitement and fear of coming to Johannesburg; the tempests of the Youth League; the endless delays of the Treason Trial; the drama of Rivonia. It was like a waking dream and I attempted to transfer it to paper as simply and truthfully as I could.

Nelson Mandela, *Long Walk to Freedom*,
pp. 415–416. 1994. Boston: Little, Brown.

Although this first draft of his memoirs was lost, the idea of recording his life story would lead to the publication of *Long Walk To Freedom* in 1994. This passage is interesting for reasons other than tracing the origins of the autobiography though. It also reveals other aspects of autobiographical writing we should think about.

Firstly, the writing is done for a purpose. There is an underlying intention°. In this case, Mandela's purpose in recording his life story was to remind people of the struggle for political liberation and to inspire a younger generation of freedom fighters. Given the purposes of the autobiography, it is not surprising that the text focuses more on public events and policies and less on the private thoughts and experiences of Nelson Rolihlahla Mandela.

A second aspect of autobiographical writing revealed here is that writing is a selective process. In the case of an autobiography, and in 'memoirs' especially, the writing relies on memory. The writer writes about what he or she remembers of the past. In the case of *Long Walk to Freedom*, the autobiography is a recollection of Mandela's past. It is also a selective portrayal of that past from his point of view. This raises interesting questions about whether autobiographies should be accepted as being absolutely true or not. People find it difficult to escape their personal preferences and biases°. An autobiography may be factual, because it records events which really happened. But it is, and has to be, a subjective° interpretation of those events. Other people might see and react to the same events in very different ways.

IN 1996 JEAN DOMINIQUE BAUBY, the chief editor for *Elle* magazine in Paris, had a massive stroke that badly damaged his brain stem. He stayed mentally fit and fully conscious, although he was completely paralyzed except for some muscles in his neck and his left eyelid. He soon realized while in hospital that people were making assumptions about him based on what they saw or heard of his condition, and that this influenced the way they behaved towards him. He wanted to show that people in his position, with 'locked-in syndrome', were still capable of thinking clearly, expressing ideas, and experiencing life. So, using a system of signals and letters, he dictated the whole of his autobiographical book *The Diving Bell and the Butterfly* by blinking his eyelid. The book is about his time in hospital and his life before and up to his stroke. It is a very moving book, and well worth reading.

AUTOBIOGRAPHY

Mandela's autobiographical writings were also edited and commented on by Walter Sisulu and Ahmed Kathrada before being finalized. This process suggests that the final text was carefully shaped or made. Autobiographies are not simply spontaneous stories about somebody's life. They are stories in which the author deliberately selects and arranges events in order to encourage the reader to see those events in particular ways.

It is impossible for an autobiography to encapsulate a whole life by telling every single detail about a person. Life is too complex and varied to permit a record of every detail. We do not remember all the events of our life with equal clarity. We do not always necessarily understand ourselves fully. Also, we never fully understand the meaning, significance° and implications of our interactions with others. Finally, we may find it difficult to speak about certain things – especially those of a deeply personal or traumatic nature – in a direct way. The act of writing an autobiography is the act of reliving the past, in terms of both its joy and its pain.

In *Long Walk to Freedom* readers are aware that certain aspects of Mandela's life are emphasized at the expense of others. Although this autobiography is a thorough account of Mandela's life, the feelings of the inner, private person are usually concealed. Thus, while the autobiography documents hardship and struggle, it only hints at the author's inner feelings. The 'I' that narrates is often emotionally distant, even though this is his life story told by himself. Personal feeling and inner anguish are partly concealed by focusing on the details of outer events and actions.

✪ Read the extract from the Rivonia Treason Trial speech again. Compare the opening words of Nelson Mandela's speech at the Rivonia Trial with this description:

KISSED AND HELD MY WIFE for the first time in all these many years. It was a moment I had dreamed about a thousand times. It was as if I were still dreaming. I held her to me for what seemed like an eternity. We were still and silent except for the sound of our hearts. I did not want to let go of her at all, but I broke free and

embraced my daughter and then took her child onto my lap. It had been twenty-one years since I had even touched my wife's hand.

Nelson Mandela, *Long Walk to Freedom*,
pp. 450–451. 1994. Boston: Little, Brown.

✪ COMPARE the personal characteristics reflected in the speech Mandela made at the Rivonia Trial with the characteristics reflected in this extract. Do the two portrayals of Mandela coincide?

✪ HOW DO YOU FEEL after reading the second extract? Try to describe what you think or feel about it.

The 'I am' statements of the Rivonia Trial are certainly factual, but they lack the emotional force of this memory of personal contact. It is on occasions like this that readers gain a glimpse into the inner person of Nelson Mandela. His joy at touching his wife for the first time in twenty-one years highlights the cruelty of his imprisonment and draws attention to the depth of human suffering. The reader gains a sense that the fight for justice does not only result in harsh conditions in prison like forced labour, poor food and brutal warders. Another significant form of suffering is the personal suffering of individuals; but this is often hidden from the public eye. Much of Mandela's pain seems to come from losing the companionship and intimacy that are part of all personal interrelationships. As readers we can probably all imagine how we would feel in a similar situation. And by thinking about how we would feel if the same things happened to us, we gain a deeper insight into the person and his life.

AUTOBIOGRAPHY

YOU ARE NOW going to write an autobiographical piece about yourself. But before you do this, we are going to look at some ideas which will help you to write more effectively.

Writing anything is difficult. There is nothing unusual in feeling apprehensive about writing. However, writing something that pleases you is wonderful. It is well worth the effort involved. To make writing easier, you can approach it step by step. Try these steps to start yourself off.

A writer's journal

One of the keys to successful writing is constant practice. The more you write, the better your writing will be. You will become used to expressing yourself in writing if you do it frequently, and by keeping a writer's journal.

A writer's journal is a blank notebook in which you write down your experiences, thoughts, ideas and impressions every day. Write whatever comes to mind. Write about your life: your family, your job, your university courses, your groceries, events in the news or anything else that you are thinking about. (You could also use your writer's journal to jot down your responses to the questions that we ask throughout this book.) Don't worry about expressing yourself 'correctly' from the start. What is more important is that you write at least half a page every day.

As you write in your journal every day, you will gradually find it easier to express yourself in writing. You will gain practice in selecting and representing facts and experiences that are significant to you and interesting to a reader. (Always remember that you are writing for an audience, even an imaginary one.) Finally, you will see that writing about your own life is a subjective° exercise. When you write your own autobiographical piece, your experience of keeping a writer's journal will help you.

2 Reasons for writing

Writing is a form of communication°. This means that you (a specific person) are writing about something (a particular topic) for someone (a specific audience). Knowing what your topic requires of you and your reasons for writing on that topic will help you to communicate your ideas more effectively. Suppose for a moment that you are to write a university assignment on a particular experience you have had. Before you begin writing, it may be helpful if you ask yourself a few questions:

These questions require you to think about yourself as the writer of the assignment.

✪ What is my position in relation to this experience? How am I involved in the experience? What did I learn from it or gain from it? Why was it important to me?

These questions deal with the topic and purpose of the assignment.

✪ What experience am I going to write about? What are the main details that I need to write down? What do I want my reader to know or understand? What impression do I want to create?

These questions point to your audience; in this case, your university lecturers.

✪ Who is going to read this piece of writing? Why are they going to read it? Do I have a casual or formal relationship with my readers?

Your answers to these questions will help you to select the material and the writing style that is most appropriate to the task that you have been asked to fulfil. We saw in the previous section that even autobiography, which we might think is the most truthful form of writing, can be written in such a way that it reflects particular positions or opinions. In *Long Walk to Freedom* we gather that Mandela's purpose is mainly political. As a result, the writing concentrates on providing a clear sense of his life and development as an ANC activist. This emphasis, in turn, means that other aspects of Nelson Mandela's life are dealt with less fully than might otherwise be the case.

Try this exercise to test how a writer's topic, purpose and audience can influence the selection of material:

✪ Choose four adjectives from the following list that you think describe you.

clever	hard-working	independent	caring
creative	attractive	competent	skilful
practical	thoughtful	understanding	careful
tolerant	diplomatic	logical	critical
fit	sporting	knowledgeable	forgiving
ambitious	persuasive	charming	friendly
sensitive	honest	persevering	energetic
decisive	domineering		

✪ Now imagine that you are describing yourself to someone you hope will become a partner in a love relationship. Which four adjectives would you choose?

✪ Next, imagine that you are describing yourself to a person you hope will employ you. Which four adjectives would you choose?

✪ Is there a difference between the sets of adjectives you chose?

You have certainly not changed much in the few seconds between answering the first and second questions, but your answer to each one probably has. This shows that we represent ourselves *differently* to *different* people according to *different* aims. Or to put it another way, our representation of ourselves changes according to our audience and our *purpose*.

3 Telling stories

Some psychologists believe that telling stories is the most profound way that humans speak about themselves. You do not have to be famous for your autobiography to be interesting. Many of the best autobiographies are about ordinary people. Jung Chang's *Wild Swans: Three Daughters of China*, for example, is about three generations of Chinese women under different forms of government. Similarly, Belinda Bozzoli's *Women of Phokeng: Consciousness, Life Strategy and Migrancy in South Africa 1900–1983* collects together the stories of poor women struggling to make a living in what is today the Northern Province in South Africa.

Now, if we asked you to write about an event in your childhood that had an especially profound impact on you, how would you go about it?

The first step is to choose the event you are going to write about. This event should be an experience that you remember in great detail (you as the writer should have a clear memory of it). It should also be an event that you think your reader will find interesting (it must be suitable for your audience). Thirdly, the event should have had a lasting effect on you, either on the way you perceive yourself and the world, or on the way you feel (the topic should deal with things which you think are important).

After you have decided on the experience you want to write about, your next step is to write down what happened to you, in the order in which you think it occurred. At this stage, you do not have to write in full sentences or perfect grammar. In the first draft of any piece of writing you should concentrate simply on getting your ideas down on paper.

Now stop and read through what you have written. Does your first draft include all the important details of the event you are describing? Will a reader be interested in reading what you have written? Telling the story of your life is more than just listing events. Readers are as interested in why things happened and how you felt about them as they are in the events themselves. Underlying causes, motives and people's personal feelings are often the most compelling aspects of any story. If you haven't written about these aspects in your first draft, try including them now.

To complete the writing of your autobiographical piece, ask yourself these questions:
✪ How will my reader feel about me once they have read my story?
✪ Do I want them to feel that way?

Depending on your answers to these questions, you might want to add descriptive words and images to your piece so that your reader can participate more fully in the experience being described. Vivid description will almost always make your writing more compelling and unique. Carefully planned, interesting writing is what will make your reader want to carry on reading. You might want to make many drafts of your piece before you feel it is finished.

Finally, when you are satisfied with your autobiographical piece, you may want to think about how you have chosen to represent yourself. Have you been absolutely truthful? Is your account an accurate version of what really happened? Do you think it's always important to be truthful and accurate? What does your own experience of writing autobiography suggest about the pitfalls and difficulties of representing 'the self'?

2 Characterization: People and Perspectives

IN CHAPTER ONE we looked at ways people represent themselves in autobiographical writing. In this chapter, we'll consider how we see and respond to the people around us. We will also explore some of the methods authors use to characterize people in their writing.

. . . .

① How are we shaping up?

Our ideas about and responses to the people we meet in the course of our lives are not based simply on their surface appearance or on our acceptance of what they claim to be. People are complex beings with many facets. We constantly judge and interpret the appearance, words and actions of the people we encounter in order to give them meaning and to decide on how we should react to them. This process of judging is influenced by the circumstances in which we view them (context°) and by the attitudes that we bring to bear upon them (perspective°). We also tend to be selective. For various reasons we emphasize certain aspects of a person's appearance and personality, while ignoring other aspects. Let's examine how this works.

Information about events and people's lives is frequently presented chronologically. This means that events are organized according to when they happened, starting with the earliest event and ending with the most recent one. Sometimes time lines are

ONE

TIME WILL TELL

used to represent events and ideas chronologically. Time lines show visually the order in which events occur and how they connect with one another.

A time line of events in South Africa over the last few decades could look like this:

● DOES THIS time line reflect any of your personal experiences?

CHARACTERIZATION

This time line presents information that applies to the lives of everybody living in South Africa during this period. The ways in which the information applies to each person may be rather general, though, because it describes the history of a country and not of individuals. Consequently, this time line cannot be said to

1923
The SANNC becomes the African National Congress (ANC).

1985–1986
State of Emergency declared in 36 magisterial districts.

1976
Soweto massacre of children protesting against use of Afrikaans in schools.

1960
Anti-Pass Laws campaigns. Sharpeville massacre.

1990
Nelson Mandela released after nearly 30 years of imprisonment.

1994
First democratic election in South Africa; Nelson Mandela becomes President.

provide a full picture of individual lives, even though it describes some of the things South Africans have experienced.

The time line for South Africa shows something about its citizens' public identity or national identity – it presents a picture of the lives of 'South Africans'. Your own time line would probably reflect an identity that is less public and more private. Try drawing a time line, filling in events from your life which you think show who you are as an individual.

A time line is a particular way of telling the story of a country or of an individual person. Time lines describe life by selecting specific experiences and details only. They cannot include all aspects of a country's history or a person's life. Certain things seem more important than others and are therefore included, while other things are excluded because they do not seem significant. By emphasizing certain aspects and ignoring others, we give a particular 'shape' to the experience or the person being described.

The links between a time line for a country and a time line for an individual should draw our attention to another important consideration. People do not live their lives in a vacuum; they are part of a wider social background and exist within particular circumstances according to time and place. Personal experience and individual behaviour need to be seen against the backdrop of history and society.

● HOW would you describe your experience of a great public event?

Any description of identity seems to be made up of gaps (what we choose to ignore) and selections (what we think is important). Time lines also do not show how individuals experience public events on a personal level. They give no indication of people's emotions or how different individuals might respond in different ways to specific circumstances.

Events in South Africa have had a profound impact on the literature that the country has produced. What does this *Madam & Eve* cartoon suggest about writing and story-telling in South Africa?

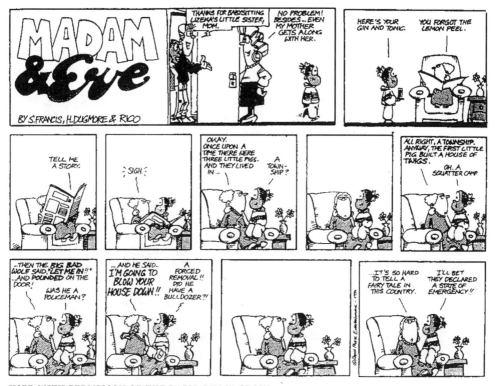

USED WITH PERMISSON OF THE RAPID PHASE GROUP

Do you agree or disagree with the idea that the only stories that can be told in South Africa are political ones? Why?

Look at me!

Even though we might see ourselves in a certain way, other people often see us completely differently. As a result, different people describe the characters of others in different ways: they characterize people differently.

'Character' can be defined as the collection of features or traits that together form the individual nature of a person or thing. The *Oxford Advanced Learner's Dictionary* defines 'character' as 'all the mental or moral qualities that make a person, group, nation, etc. different from others'. To characterize someone would then be to talk about an individual's identity in a way that typifies them or allows us to speak of them as unique. The dictionary entries for characterize and characterization appear like this:

> **characterize, -ise** /ˈkærəktəraɪz/ *v* **1 (a)** to be typical or characteristic of sb/sth: [Vn] *the rolling hills that characterize this part of England.* **(b)** (esp passive) to give sb/sth their most noticeable quality or feature: [Vn] *His work is characterized by its imagery and humour.* **2** ~ **sb/sth (as sth)** to describe or show the character(1) of sb/sth as sth: [Vn-adj] *The novelist characterizes his heroine as capricious and passionate.* [Vnadv] *How would you characterize the mood of the 1980s?* [also Vn-n].
> ▶ **characterization, -isation** /ˌkærəktəraɪˈzeɪʃn/ *n* [U] the action or process of characterizing (CHARACTERIZE 2), esp the description of human character in novels, plays, etc: *Mark Twain's skill at characterization.*

We tend to think that people have particular characteristics. A certain physical characteristic that we notice in somebody often becomes closely linked with the way we think about that person. Sometimes a noticeable characteristic of this sort becomes so much a part of how we think about the person that we see it as part of the person's character. A physical feature that becomes part of someone's characterization is described in this anecdote:

MY FATHER has smoked all his life. As a result he has a smoker's cough. If he is in a public place he has a particular way of trying to disguise his cough so that it does not disturb other people. As a little girl, if I got lost in a crowd, all I had to do was stand still and listen. Sure enough, I would be able to hear the sound of his cough and that would guide me to him.

But when we think and talk about character, we refer to far more than a person's physical characteristics. Psychological, ethical and moral qualities also become part of the way in which we characterize a person. Psychological qualities are those that relate to a person's personality, which would include the way someone thinks, feels and acts. Ethics and morals relate to various belief systems and ideas about right and wrong which affect people's behaviour. These aspects also form part of the ideas we form of somebody's character.

If we describe a person by referring only to one characteristic, then such a description is limited. It cannot encompass all the complexities° of a person's character. Also, the person we describe might see our characterization as inaccurate. They might have a completely different view of their own characteristics.

LANGUAGE, RACE AND COLOUR

In chapter one we defined a stereotype° as a fixed and standardized version of a person or a group of people. Stereotypes are often associated with prejudice and do not reflect reality. One kind of stereotyping is racial stereotyping, which involves thinking that all people of a certain ethnic or cultural group have similar traits. Stereotyped ideas about people can influence the way we expect them to behave and the way we behave towards them.

Language use reflects stereotyping. In English, the colour 'white' often has positive connotations while the colour 'black' is frequently negative. In fairy tales from various parts of the world the wicked wizard or witch is often dressed in black, while the innocent and beautiful princess wears flowing white robes. If we say that a character has 'dark thoughts', we mean that the person is evil. If we say a situation 'brightens', we mean that it improves.

Some of the negative senses in which the word 'black' appears in English are:

blacklist	black sheep	black market
blackmail	black magic	

And some of the positive uses of 'white' include:

white magic	pure white	whiter than white
knight on a white horse	white lie	

Can you think of expressions in which 'white' is used to refer to something negative, and 'black' to something positive? The difficulty in thinking of such reversals shows us how strong these language stereotypes are.

Here are some positive uses of 'black', and some negative uses of 'white':

black belt (karate)
black gold (oil)
in the black (to not owe money)
black tie (formal clothes)

white elephant (something that is not useful)
white flag (surrender)
whitewash (make something seem acceptable by hiding the truth)

If you can speak another language, try to think of the connotations of these colours in that language. Are these connotations similar to or different from the connotations they have in English?

Here is an extract from the opening paragraph of an autobiography by the writer R. K. Narayan. Think about what Narayan valued in his life and whether his grandmother had the same ideas as he did about what was important.

 LL DAY LONG, I sat half buried in sand piled in a corner of our garden, raising castles and mountain-ranges, unaware of the fierce Madras sun overhead. I had a peacock and a monkey for company. The monkey was chained to a post, on top of which a little cabin was available for his shelter, but he preferred to sit on the roof of his home, hanging down his tail. He responded to the name of Rama by baring his teeth, and kept a wary eye on the peacock ... I cannot say exactly when they came into my life, but they seemed to have been always there with me. In an early photo of myself, when I was four years old, I am set [sitting] on a miniature bamboo chair flanked by the peacock and the monkey. ... I was proud of the group in the picture and hoped that others would see a resemblance between me and Rama. When I sought confirmation on this point, my grandmother was horrified and said, 'What a fool to want to look like a monkey! You are in bad company. You must send away that creature. Wanting to look like a monkey when God has endowed you with such large eyes and all those curls falling down your cheeks!' She was so fond of my curls that she never let a barber come near me, which means that I had constantly to part the veil of hair with my fingers when I wished to look at anyone.

FROM: R. K. Narayan, *My Days: A Memoir*,
pp. 1–2. 1989. London: Penguin.

Narayan's grandmother is upset because he thinks he looks like the monkey. Although he likes the idea of looking like a monkey, his grandmother finds the idea horrifying! This conflict between the way Narayan sees himself and his grandmother's ideal picture of him shows that the ideas people have about identity and personality often seem to be based on those aspects of a person they value most. Narayan's grandmother values his eyes and curly hair, which she finds beautiful. She has a particular picture (or image) of him in her mind because of these features.

The values and expectations that we bring to bear upon people often determine how we respond to them and how we interpret their lives. Like Narayan's grandmother, adults often have particular ideas about a child's identity and character based on their physical and psychological development. For instance, they may say that a baby who talks a little bit earlier than expected is very intelligent. They might decide that various milestones (such as recognizing colours or learning to count) mean something important about a child's character and its future abilities as an adult ('Oh, he'll be artistic!' or 'Oh, she'll be an accountant like her father!'). Often, these predictions become simply the stories that parents tell about their children: they become part of the way they understand and describe their children's personalities. Later on, other events become part of these stories, such as going to school, having accidents, falling in love or starting a job. All these things shape our understanding of who a person is when they become part of the stories we tell about each other.

Think back to your own childhood.

✪ Many children love stories about when their parents were young. Are there stories about your parents' young days that you enjoy?
✪ What stories do your parents tell about your childhood?
✪ Perhaps you identified so strongly with your parents that you wanted to be just like them. In what ways did you want to be like your parents when you were a child? In what ways do you still want to be like them?
✪ How have your parents influenced your own personality and ideals?

The following poem was written during the period that preceded the release of Nelson Mandela, when many people died in violence in South Africa. Funerals were very important to the politics of the time, since such occasions became opportunities for expressing protest against the apartheid regime.

THE DANCER
Gcina Mhlophe

Mama,
they tell me you were a dancer
they tell me you had long
beautiful legs to carry your graceful body
they tell me you were a dancer

Mama,
they tell me you sang beautiful solos
they tell me you closed your eyes
always when the feeling of the song
was right, and lifted your face to the sky
they tell me you were an enchanting dancer

Mama,
they tell me you were always so gentle
they talk of a willow tree
swaying lovingly over clear running water
in early Spring when they talk of you
they tell me you were a slow dancer

Mama,
they tell me you were a wedding dancer
they tell me you smiled and closed your eyes
your arms curving outward just a little
and your feet shuffling in the sand;
tshi tshi tshitshitshitha, tshitshi tshitshitshitha
o hee! how I wish I was there to see you
they tell me you were a pleasure to watch

Mama
they tell me I am a dancer too
but I don't know ...
I don't know for sure what a wedding dancer is
there are no more weddings
but many, many funerals
where we sing and dance
running fast with the coffin
of a would-be bride or would-be groom
strange smiles have replaced our tears
our eyes are full of vengeance, Mama

Dear, dear Mama,
they tell me I am a funeral dancer.

REPRINTED BY PERMISSION:
Gcina Mhlophe.

Let's think about how the mother and daughter are characterized
in the poem.
- ✪ The first four stanzas of the poem deal with stories that people
  tell the daughter about her mother as a dancer. Write a short
  paragraph in which you describe the mother as a dancer.
- ✪ How do you think the daughter feels about the way other
  people characterize her mother? Does she admire her and
  identify with her? That is, does she want to be a dancer just like
  her mother was?
- ✪ How does the daughter represent herself in the poem? What
  information about herself does she select to give to readers?
- ✪ How do you think the daughter feels about being a funeral
  dancer and not a wedding dancer?
- ✪ To what extent is the daughter's character shaped by the
  political events that surround her?

TWO

CONSIDERING CHARACTER

IN THIS SECTION we will examine in more detail how context and perspective influence characterization.

 Context

The entry for 'context' in the *Oxford Advanced Learner's Dictionary* gives two possible meanings for the word, depending on how it is used:

> **context** /ˈkɒntekst/ *n* [C,U] **1** words that come before and after a word, phrase, statement, etc, helping to show what its meaning is: *Can't you guess the meaning of the word from the context?* ○ *Don't quote my words **out of context*** (eg so as to mislead people about what I mean). **2** circumstances in which sth happens or in which sth is to be considered: *In the context of the present economic crisis it seems unwise to lower taxes.* ○ *You have to see these changes in context: they're part of a larger plan.*
> ▶ **contextual** /kənˈtekstʃuəl/ *adj* of or according to context: *Contextual clues can help one to find the meaning.* **contextually** *adv.*

The first definition refers to the use of the word 'context' when discussing language. But in this section we are more interested in the second sense, where 'context' refers to the circumstances in which things happen and are thought about.

People behave differently in different circumstances. While certain aspects of our characters are carried over from one situation to another, we can imagine ourselves in situations in which our behaviour would bring out only certain characteristics. We would not expect people, for example, to behave exactly the same as they would normally when they are under extreme pressure. We cannot, therefore, claim that character is always constant. Character changes according to circumstance and we cannot speak of character without taking into account the context in which we see a particular individual act.

The same is true for characters in literature (in novels or plays, for example). Literary texts depict characters in particular circumstances. We cannot assume that the character would behave in exactly the same way in other circumstances. The literary character is a created 'person' acting in a context established by the plot and the other characters in the work. We always need to take account of the context. Certain aspects or characteristics of a character may emerge more clearly in some circumstances (contexts) than in others. Remember too that any character in a literary work exists as a part of the work. He or she might be created as a point of comparison for other characters or might be created to advance some aspect of the plot. Literary characters should always be seen in terms of the literary work of which they are a part.

Another difficulty exists when speaking of characters in literary texts. Just as we need, at times, to put texts in their social and historical context to understand them more fully, so characters often need to be seen as being representative of their society and time. We would take a different view of a character in a novel set in eighteenth-century Nigeria, for example, than one in twentieth-century New York, even if they behaved in the 'same' way. The social and historical context of the work is thus essential to our understanding of a character, and we cannot wrench characters from their context and still interpret the action of the work meaningfully.

Perspective

As readers and observers, we always see things and interpret them from a particular point of view or perspective. The *Oxford Advanced Learner's Dictionary* defines perspective like this:

> **perspective** /pə'spektɪv/ *n* **1** [U] the art of drawing solid objects on a flat surface so as to give the right impression of their height, width, depth and position in relation to each other: *a perspective drawing* ○ *The artist shows a fine command of perspective.* ⇨ picture. **2** [C] a view¹(2), esp one stretching into the distance: *get a perspective of the whole valley.* **3** [C] a particular attitude towards sth; a point of view (POINT¹): *see things from a global/ feminist/Christian perspective* ○ *gain a different perspective on the problem* ○ *keep a sense of perspective* (ie see things in a balanced way).

In order to save space and make entries efficient, dictionaries use a variety of abbreviations to give information about a word. In a dictionary entry, sth stands for 'something' and sb for 'somebody'. There are a number of other abbreviations you will encounter; your dictionary should explain its abbreviations in its opening pages, or sometimes at the bottom of each page. The *Oxford Advanced Learner's Dictionary* lists its abbreviations in the front cover and on the first page.

The first sense of 'perspective' in the dictionary definition relates to the word as it is used in visual art. When we talk about perspective in art we look at the way physical objects appear in relation to each other. Perspective relates to the angle from which we look at a scene. The objects that are further away are usually represented as smaller than those that are close by. An artist drawing a picture of a landscape will probably consider perspective in order to ensure that the picture looks realistic.

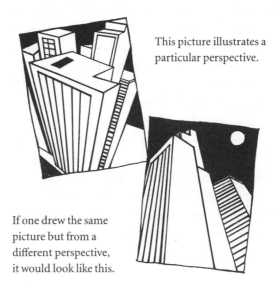

This picture illustrates a particular perspective.

If one drew the same picture but from a different perspective, it would look like this.

Now that we see the picture from a different angle, some of the objects look slightly different. When we talk about perspective in relation to the physical world, we are referring to how the place or position from which we look affects what we see before us.

In the second sense 'perspective' is a synonym for 'view'. It relates to what an observer might see of the physical world from a particular position. Someone standing on top of a hill on a clear day would have a good view of the countryside that lies below.

The third meaning of perspective, that it is 'a particular attitude towards something; a point of view', relates to the sense in which we generally speak of perspective in this book. In the illustrations above, we showed that the way in which we see the world changes according to the position from which we view it. The same is true about the way we see people: if we see them from a different point of view, through the eyes of someone else, for instance, we might characterize them differently.

Whenever we tell a story we adopt a particular perspective. In discussing literary texts we refer to the 'voice' that tells the story as the 'narrator'; the narrator tells us, the readers, the story. Events and characters are presented from the narrator's perspective.

However, narration occurs in different forms or styles. Literary critics have traditionally spoken about narrative in terms of 'first-person' or 'third-person' narration. These terms are used to describe the perspective from which a story is told. When the narrator is a participant or character in the story, we describe him or her as a 'first-person narrator'. A first-person narrator can usually be identified by his or her use of the pronoun 'I'. The fact that the storyteller is one of the characters means that the perspective from which the story is told is the perspective of that character. It is important to remember that a first-person narrator does not necessarily have the same identity as the author. In fiction, the 'I' is a character invented by the author. The narrator should not be confused with the author, since the ideas, experiences and characteristics of the narrator can easily be completely different from those of the author. On the other hand, in autobiographical writing, the author and the 'I' who tells the story are the same person.

Third-person narration refers to the way a story is told from the perspective of someone who is not one of the characters. The narrator in this case is outside the story and not a participant in its events. For example, I might wish to write a story assuming that I can see into the minds of all of my characters; the way I wrote the story would be based on the idea that I know exactly what my characters think and feel. The narration is not limited to a particular character's perspective. This type of narrator is a 'third-person' or 'omniscient' narrator. 'Omniscience' refers to the idea that someone 'knows everything'. An omniscient narrator, therefore, presents the story from a perspective where he or she seems to know everything about the characters and their world. As readers, we can only know what we are told by the narrator with regard to characters' thoughts, feelings and motivations. If an omniscient narrator presents us with a full and detailed picture of events and characters, we often tend to accept the narrator's perspective as our own. In other words, we tend to see the characters from the narrator's point of view and to share the narrator's opinion about the characters.

When we think about the 'voice' narrating a story, we need to think carefully about objectivity. A first-person narrator is most likely to offer a very subjective account. If the story is being told by a character, we have to take into account that he or she has particular interests, ideas, capacities and beliefs which will influence how the story is told. We might have to be very careful about taking the narrator's word as an objective or reliable interpretation of things.

But this problem is not limited only to first-person narration. On the face of it, a third-person or omniscient narrator should be more objective. However, it is important to note that this is not always the case. A third-person narrator may choose to focus on the thoughts, feelings and actions of one character only, and so foreground that character and his or her point of view. One effect of this narrative technique is that the reader is encouraged to sympathize with the character whose perspective is presented. Similarly, the narrator's opinions and world-view might affect the way in which she or he describes people. For example, if the narrator admires an aspect of a character's behaviour or personality, the description of that person will usually influence us to share the narrator's opinion. In the same way, a negative description from the narrator would affect our feelings about events or characters.

Narrative perspective is a central aspect of understanding and thinking about a literary work. In poetry, as in novels, we cannot assume that the ideas, attitudes and events shown in the poem are a direct expression of the poet's own life and experience. The 'voice' that speaks in the poem – the 'I' that narrates the poem – could be a character created by the poet to express a particular viewpoint or perspective. The ideas and feelings expressed in the poem may differ from those of the person who makes the poem. Although there might be significant similarities between the ideas and experiences of the writer and the situation described in the text, we cannot assume that they are identical. For this reason we refer to the voice in a poem as the 'speaker'. This allows us to think of the writer and the text as separate from each other.

In the poem which follows, we do not know whether the 'I' is a man or a woman. We also do not know whether the piece is auto-biographical. Therefore, we refer to the 'I' as the speaker. The poem explores two people's differing perspectives in relation to a particular situation. Before reading the poem, think about the following questions:

✪ Do you and your parents attach the same importance to the same things?

✪ Think of the attitudes of your friends and family to university education and, more specifically, to the subjects you are study-ing. Which careers and subjects do you consider important? Why? Which subjects do they consider important?

✪ How do you feel about the difference between what you con-sider important and what your family and friends consider important? Do these differences sometimes cause conflict and hurt? Why?

POEM FOR MY MOTHER
Jennifer Davids

That isn't everything, you said
on the afternoon I brought a poem
to you hunched over the washtub
with your hands
the shrivelled
burnt granadilla
skin of your hands
covered by foam.

And my words
slid like a ball
of hard blue soap
into the tub
to be grabbed and used by you
to rub the clothes.

A poem isn't all
there is to life, you said
with your blue-ringed gaze
scanning the page
once looking over my shoulder
and back at the immediate
dirty water

and my words
being clenched
smaller and
smaller.

FROM: *Searching for Words.*
1974. Cape Town: David Philip.

✪ Do you think the speaker in the poem is a man or a woman?
  Why do you think so?
✪ The words 'I', 'my' and 'you' are used in the poem several times
  and draw attention to the kind of relationship that exists
  between the two characters. What is this relationship?
✪ Do you think the mother and the speaker are in conflict with
  each other in this situation? Why?
✪ How do you think the speaker would like the mother to react
  to the poem that is shown to her?
✪ The mother's position is described as 'hunched'. What does the
  word 'hunched' mean? What does it tell us about the mother?
✪ The skin of the mother's hands is compared to granadilla skin.
  What does this suggest about her and her work?
✪ The third stanza describes the mother's reaction to the poem.
  Describe her reaction in your own words. Judging by this reac-
  tion, how do you think the mother feels about the speaker's
  poem?
✪ What does the poet's choice of the words 'grabbed' and 'used'
  imply about the mother's attitude to the poem and to things in
  general?
✪ What do the mother's words 'A poem isn't all / there is to life'
  reveal about the importance she attaches to the poem? Which

other actions of the mother confirm the attitude she reveals by these words?

✪ Read the last stanza. How important is the poem to the speaker? How does the speaker feel about the fact that the mother does not pay attention to the poem?

✪ Why do you think the lines become shorter towards the end of the poem? What does this process of shortening the lines suggest about the way the speaker feels?

In 'Poem for my mother' we can see two different perspectives on the value of the poem that the speaker shows the mother. To the speaker, the poem is important. It is something valuable to give to the mother. The mother, however, does not see it in the same way. As a result, the speaker feels hurt and rejected.

Imagine that the speaker wrote a letter about this incident:

Dear Mother

Yesterday afternoon I tried to show you the first poem that I ever wrote. You paid it no attention and I was deeply hurt. What hurt me, perhaps more than your indifference, was the fact that you didn't realize how much showing it to you meant to me. I had really hoped to show you the person I had become, in no small measure as a result of your care over the years. Now we seem to inhabit such different worlds.

While I will always respect you and all that you have done for me, I am so sorry that I cannot share the other sides of myself and my life with you.

All my love

TIME OFF
TO WRITE!

Imagine that you are the mother. Write a letter to the speaker to explain your reaction to the poem. Try to make the speaker understand your behaviour.

As in 'Poem for my mother', writers often present different perspectives on the same events and issues. The style of their writing and the information they include reveal what they consider important. Next we'll read how different writers characterize one man, Andrew Grove, from different perspectives.

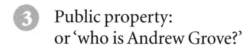

3 Public property:
or 'who is Andrew Grove?'

Each year the American magazine TIME decides that someone deserves to be the 'Man of the Year'. The editors of the magazine select people who are admired for making a particularly important discovery, or people who have acted in ways that have had an impact on many others. From this group they choose one person to whom they give the title of 'Man of the Year'. This shows that the magazine believes this person has had a profound effect on public life, in America or in another part of the world, during the previous year. In 1997 the person chosen for this title was Andrew Grove. He was selected because he runs the company Intel, which manufactures 90 per cent of the computer microchips used in the world.

TELLING HIS STORIES

The magazine has an interesting way of presenting the character of Andrew Grove. Instead of writing one article dealing with Andrew Grove, they provide the accounts or stories of more than one writer. We, the audience, read each person's idea of who Andrew Grove is and what he is like as a person. From these accounts, each reader forms their own impression of Andrew Grove's character. Does Andrew Grove see himself as a hero? Is he really the most important man in the world? Does he fulfil our expectations of what a 'Man of the Year' should be like?

The following extracts are adapted from the TIME magazine articles about Andrew Grove. Although he is a real person, in these extracts Andrew Grove is rather like a character in a story or a play. People seem to see him in different ways. As you read through the articles, think about Andrew Grove's identity: who is Andrew Grove? What different kinds of information do the articles give us about him?

MAN OF THE YEAR

... driven by the passion of Intel's Andrew Grove

by Walter Isaacson

THIS HAS BEEN A YEAR OF BIG STORIES, including the death of Princess Diana. But the story that had the most impact on 1997 was the one that had the most impact throughout this decade: the growth of a new global economy. This has been propelled by the power of the microchip.

And so TIME chooses as its 1997 Man of the Year Andrew Grove, chairman and CEO of Intel, the person most responsible for the growth in the power and innovative potential of microchips. His character traits are emblematic of this amazing century: a paranoia bred from his having been a refugee from the Nazis and then from the Communists; an entrepreneurial optimism instilled as an immigrant to a land brimming with freedom and opportunity; and a sharpness tinged with arrogance that comes from being a brilliant mind on the front line of a revolution.

The steel in his character comes through. He has a courageous passion mixed with an engineer's analytical coldness, whether it be in battling his prostate cancer or in guiding Intel's death-defying climb to dominate the market for the world's most important product.

These traits have allowed Grove to push with paranoiac obsession the bounds of innovation and to build Intel, which makes 90 per cent of the planet's PC microprocessors, into a company worth $115 billion. One reason for this is because Grove believes that we will continually find new things for microchips to do that we could hardly imagine even two years before.

The dawn of a new millennium – which is the grandest measure we have of human time – permits us to think about history. We can pause to notice what Grove calls the points when new circumstances alter the way the world works. These can happen because of inventions such as the microchip, an advance which propels a new economy. Its impact on growth and productivity numbers is still a matter of dispute, but not its impact on the way we work and live.

ADAPTED FROM: TIME,
29 December 1997 – 5 January 1998

✪ What reasons does this journalist give as to why Andrew Grove deserves the title of 'Man of the Year'?
✪ Make a list of the characteristics of Andrew Grove that this journalist sees as important.
✪ Do you personally admire the characteristics that this journalist appears to admire?

A Survivor's Tale

by *Joshua Cooper Ramo*

BUDAPEST: DECEMBER 1956. The Red Army had been streaming into the city for a month, brutalizing Hungary's October revolution. The foggy nights, filled before with the cries of ecstatic students, were now split with the sound of machinery – Soviet tanks. Fear blossomed in the dampness. The Premier disappeared.

The boy – lean, strikingly handsome – hoped the trouble would pass. During the day he buried himself in schoolwork. Nights he passed at home. But over his books, across his strong Hungarian coffee, he heard rumours: the Russians were rounding up students. Children were disappearing. Trains were leaving for the frontier.

He longed to ignore the stories. He had already lived through the horror of the Nazis, outsmarting the SS death squads. Boys at school mocked him before the war because he was a Jew. After the war they mocked him because his father was a businessman and so a capitalist. In his government file the boy was already an 'enemy of the classes.' He wasn't going to wait for the Soviets.

So he ran. With his best school friend he hopped on a train westward, as close to the Austrian border as they dared. The Russians were storming through the countryside, arresting everyone they could. The two boys would have to race the Red Army to the border. And since no one would guide them, they gathered the last of their money, the last of their courage, and bought directions from a hunchbacked smuggler who spoke of secret byways the Russians had not yet discovered.

And so, hours later, he found himself face down in a muddy field somewhere near the Austrian border – but how near? Soldiers marched by, dogs barked. Then a voice cried out, in Hungarian, the words paralysing him with fear:

'Who is there?' Even forty years later, as he laughs at the memory, his eyes harden; he shifts his neck under his collar. Had the smuggler betrayed him? 'We thought, "this is it!"' The man shouted again. Now at the limits of his courage, the boy finally answered: 'Where are we?' 'Austria,' came the reply. The relief poured cool as the rain. Andras Grof, a name he would later Americanize to Andrew Grove, stood up and picked his way towards the future.

It is hard to imagine the components of greatness, but surely survival is among their number. And Andrew Grove has always been, if nothing else, a survivor. From that terrifying night, Grove, 61, has been pushed by a will to live as other men are fired by a taste for power or money. Intel, the firm that Grove built, has survived in one of the most tumultuous industries in history. Grove says: 'Only the paranoid survive.'

Grove believes in relentless change and fearless leadership. Yet, he insists, 'I haven't changed.' He is a protective father of two daughters (he has asked us not to reveal their names or occupations). He is also a teacher at Stanford University. He teaches there part-time and his courses are extremely popular. And he is worth more than $300 million.

At work he operates from the same kind of cubicle as everyone else at the company gets. But Grove is not all work: he skis, bikes with his wife Eva, listens to opera. He occasionally breaks out into a wild, disjointed dance (his kids call it groving instead of grooving). The dance step is typical: Grove is a passionate if disjointed man. He is a famously tough manager, who late at night can still fill Intel's offices with a rolling laugh. He is a man who lost most of his hearing when he was young, but who soldiered through the toughest science classes flawlessly by lip reading and compulsive study. 'Ruthless intellectual honesty' is the way friends describe Grove's strongest characteristic. Andy has another word for it: 'Fear'.

ADAPTED FROM: TIME, 29 December 1997 – 5 January 1998

CHARACTERIZATION

- Although this article is also about Andrew Grove, it is set in a different context to the first article. Describe the differences between the articles.
- Make a list of the character traits of Andrew Grove on which the writer of this article focuses. Do these qualities influence our understanding of Andrew Grove as he was presented in the first article?
- If you were Andrew Grove's daughter and you were interviewed by journalists about him, which of his qualities would you describe?
- Use the information in the extracts to draw a time line for Andrew Grove.
- Do you feel that this time line gives you a clearer idea of who this man is? Does the information in the time line answer the question 'Who is Andrew Grove?' or does it leave out ideas that are important?
- Look back on your own life. Are there things that you were once ashamed of, but about which you now feel confident or proud? Write a short passage contrasting different stages in your development.

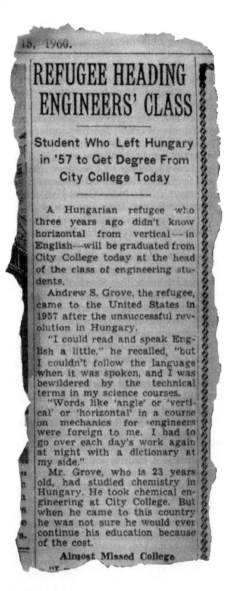

15, 1960.

REFUGEE HEADING ENGINEERS' CLASS

Student Who Left Hungary in '57 to Get Degree From City College Today

A Hungarian refugee who three years ago didn't know horizontal from vertical — in English — will be graduated from City College today at the head of the class of engineering students.

Andrew S. Grove, the refugee, came to the United States in 1957 after the unsuccessful revolution in Hungary.

"I could read and speak English a little," he recalled, "but I couldn't follow the language when it was spoken, and I was bewildered by the technical terms in my science courses.

"Words like 'angle' or 'vertical' or 'horizontal' in a course on mechanics for engineers were foreign to me. I had to go over each day's work again at night with a dictionary at my side."

Mr. Grove, who is 23 years old, had studied chemistry in Hungary. He took chemical engineering at City College. But when he came to this country he was not sure he would ever continue his education because of the cost.

Almost Missed College

"I

WRITING LIFE

The extracts from articles on Andrew Grove show how different writers consider various aspects of his life and personality, and characterize him in different ways. Writers of novels sometimes use the same techniques and choose to characterize the characters in their novels by portraying them from different perspectives. That is, they let the reader 'see' different aspects of the characters through the eyes of certain characters.

One of the earliest novels written in English was published in the 1760s by Laurence Sterne. At the time the book was highly controversial and was denounced by many leading figures of the day for moral and literary reasons. The title of the novel is *The Life and Opinions of Tristram Shandy*. It presents a picture of the fictional character named Tristram Shandy. Or at least, that is what it almost does – in fact, the book says very little about the life of the character and does not reveal much about his opinions either. Instead, it focuses extensively on other characters who spend time with Tristram Shandy, and reveals quite a lot about the author's personality. One of the many interesting things about this book is what this says about writing about the self and identity. To me, it seems that the very difficulty of describing a 'self' is shown by the way in which the book is 'about' a self who is so seldom revealed. But more than this, the author also examines the question of when a 'self' begins. The book begins by stating that it is necessary to describe the moment at which Tristram Shandy was conceived if it is going to talk about the life of Tristram Shandy. In other words, the problem of a 'self' is taken back to the time before that self was born.

ISSUES RELATING to the intricacies of perspective and characterization are of course not limited to these two novels. Among the huge number of texts which explore issues similar to these are *David Copperfield* by Charles Dickens, *Great Expectations*, also by Charles Dickens, *The Great Gatsby* by F. Scott Fitzgerald, and *The Catcher in the Rye* by J. D. Salinger. Reading any of them would provide many opportunities for exploring these concepts further.

Many other books also explore this problem, though in a different way. One example is Salman Rushdie's novel *Midnight's Children*, which was first published in 1982. In this novel, the opening scenes focus on the character Saleem. He starts to describe his own identity in terms of the moment of his birth, which he claims as very important to his identity, although he then goes on to revise even this. Within the next few paragraphs, he characterizes his identity in different terms by saying that who he is depends on events and people that precede his birth. His 'self' is, in a way, 'made' by these factors, as they contribute to the way that he understands himself and to the stories he tells people about himself and his identity.

IN THIS SECTION we are going to apply the ideas and concepts of characterization, context and perspective that we explored in the previous two sections to a short story by Can Themba called 'The Suit'.

THREE

DRESSED TO KILL?
CAN THEMBA'S 'THE SUIT'

 ## Reading the text

In chapter one we suggested you preview a text to get a general impression of its content by means of skimming and scanning. We noted that good readers often skim through a text and note the most important ideas before reading it more intensively. When you have discovered the main ideas of a text and are satisfied that you understand its basic content, you can begin to look at it in more detail to find its main ideas, arguments and themes.

> ✪ The main idea is the most important idea in each paragraph.
> ✪ The argument of a text is the way in which ideas are arranged logically in a text to make a certain point.
> ✪ The themes are the abstract ideas behind the arguments.

Often, if we list the main ideas in a text, we can produce a summary of the argument; that is, we can make a list of how the ideas are arranged in the text. The themes of the text might give us an indication of the writer's purpose and intention. Good readers, however, do not necessarily believe everything that they read. Instead, they read critically° and think about the writer's purpose, intention and tone in writing the text. Does the writer want to inform the reader? Does the writer perhaps aim at persuading the reader to do something or to think about something in a certain way? Can we infer° the writer's and/or the narrator's opinion from what is said and from the way in which it is said? Very often, the writer's purpose in writing the text and his or her opinions about the topic are veiled. The writer does not tell the reader explicitly why they are writing and how they are feeling, which is why we should read critically and carefully. Readers can get clues about the writer's or narrator's intentions and opinions by focusing on emotive words that are used in the text. Some words have strong emotional connotations. Emotive words are often used in advertisements, for instance, because they are effective in persuading people to buy a product.

Writers might seem to be writing objectively and giving factual information. However, if we look at the words they choose to describe people or situations, we see that the writing is also, in many ways, subjective.

✪ Compare the following sentences. As you read the second sentence, identify the emotive words in it. What do you think the narrator intends to convey to the reader by using these words?

Evelyn has been an English teacher for the past ten years.	The one and only Miss Evelyn Jones, a rather senior member of staff, has been a strict and effective English teacher for the past decade – though her influence on students will probably be felt for many decades to come.

✪ What images of Evelyn Jones do the writers of these sentences wish the reader to form? In the second sentence, what does the speaker suggest about her influence? In other words, do we see her influence as positive or negative when we read this description of her?

In literature, writers exploit language in every possible way to make readers interpret their stories and characters in certain ways. If we read critically to identify their emphasis, tone and use of emotive words, and if we question their purpose, we will get a clearer idea of the events and characters that writers describe.

'The Suit' is about a failing relationship between a husband and wife. Thinking about how you would behave in similar circumstances can help you to understand the story and your response to it more clearly.

- ✪ Have you ever been involved in a relationship in which your partner cheated on you? If so, how did you discover that the person was dishonest to you and had another lover? How did you feel?
- ✪ Even if you have not had such an experience, how do you imagine you would feel if you discovered that your partner had been unfaithful to you?
- ✪ If your partner was having an affair with another person, would you prefer your friends to tell you about it, or would you rather not know? Why?
- ✪ Would you consider taking revenge on your partner and the lover? Why? Do you think revenge would make you feel better about the whole matter in the long run?

BIOGRAPHICAL INFORMATION

Can Themba was born in Marabastad, Pretoria, in 1924. He studied at the University of Fort Hare and later worked in Johannesburg as an English teacher and a journalist on *Drum* and the *Golden City Post*. After being declared a banned person by the National Party government, he left for Swaziland in 1963 and died there in Manzini in 1968.

INFORMATION FROM: David Adey et al., *Companion to South African Literature*, p. 195. 1986. Johannesburg: A. D. Donker Publishers

THE SETTING OF 'THE SUIT'

The setting of a novel or play is the place in which the action happens. 'The Suit' is set in Sophiatown, which was a freehold area in Johannesburg where black people were legally able to own property, even into the early years of apartheid. Unlike the other racially divided suburbs of the time, people from different racial groups lived there. The suburb had a vibrant culture where jazz and other local music and poetry were written and performed. The people who lived there loved Sophiatown passionately, and it featured in many poems, short stories and autobiographies. However, in the mid-1950s Sophiatown was bulldozed under the regime of H. F. Verwoerd and re-classified as a white area called Triomf (Afrikaans for 'Triumph'). With the political changes of the 1990s, Triomf became known again by its original name, Sophiatown.

The Suit

Can Themba

IVE-THIRTY IN THE MORNING, and the candlewick bedspread frowned as the man under it stirred. He did not like to wake his wife lying by his side – as yet – so he crawled up and out by careful peristalsis.◇ But before he tiptoed out of his room with shoes and socks under his arm, he leaned over and peered at the sleeping serenity◇ of his wife: to him a daily matutinal miracle.◇

He grinned and yawned simultaneously, offering his wordless *Te Deum* ◇ to whatever gods for the goodness of life; for the pure beauty of his wife; for the strength surging through his willing body; for the even, unperturbed rhythms of his passage through days and months and years – it must be – to heaven.[1]

Then he slipped soundlessly into the kitchen. He flipped aside the curtain of the kitchen window, and saw outside a thin drizzle, the type that can soak one to the skin, and that could go on for days and days. He wondered, head aslant, why the rain in Sophiatown always came in the morning when workers had to creep out of their burrows; and then at how

◇ Peristalsis is the muscular contractions of the digestive system. In this context, it describes a way of moving, similar to that of a worm.

◇ This is how Philemon sees his wife. 'Serenity' means 'calm' and 'tranquil'. It suggests a religious quality.

◇ Morning miracle, connected to the 'holiness' idea suggested by the word 'serenity'.

◇ A *Te Deum* is a prayer or hymn in praise of God.

1 Philemon thinks his life is 'good' and his wife is 'pure' and 'beautiful'. For this reason he is grateful for his life. Do you think his reasons for happiness are wise?

CHARACTERIZATION

blistering heatwaves came during the day when messengers had to run errands all over; and then at how the rain came back when workers knocked off and had to scurry home.

He smiled at the odd caprice of the heavens, and tossed his head at the naughty incongruity, as if, 'Ai, but the gods!'

From behind the kitchen door, he removed an old rain cape, peeling off in places, and swung it over his head. He dashed for the lavatory, nearly slipping in a pool of muddy water, but he reached the door.[2] Aw, blast, someone had made it before him. Well, that is the toll of staying in a yard where twenty ... thirty other people have to share the same lean-to. He was dancing and burning in that climactic moment when trouser-fly will not come wide soon enough. He stepped round the lavatory and watched the streamlets of rainwater quickly wash away the jet of tension that spouted from him. The infinite after-relief. Then he dashed back to his kitchen. He grabbed the old baby-bathtub hanging on a nail under the slight shelter of the garden roof-edge. He opened a large wooden box and quickly filled the bathtub with coal. Then he inched his way back to the kitchen door and inside.[3]

He was huh-huh-huhing one of those fugitive tunes that cannot be hidden, but often just occur and linger naggingly in the head. The fire he was making soon licked up cheerfully, in mood with his contentment.[4]

2 What kind of life does this sentence describe? This description of Philemon's surroundings in Sophiatown does not seem to match Philemon's ideas about the quality of his own life. What conflict can you identify here?

3 What does this description reveal about the living conditions in Sophiatown?

4 Despite his circumstances, Philemon remains positive and content.

He had a trick for these morning chores. When the fire in the old stove warmed up, the water kettle humming on it, he gathered and laid ready the things he would need for the day: briefcase and the files that go with it; the book that he was reading currently; the letters of his lawyer boss which he usually posted before he reached the office; his wife's and his own dry-cleaning slips for the Sixty-Minutes; his lunch tin solicitously° prepared the night before by his attentive wife; and, today, the battered rain cape. By the time the kettle on the stove sang (before it actually boiled), he poured water from it into a washbasin, refilled and replaced it on the stove. Then he washed himself carefully: across the eyes, under, in and out the armpits, down the torso and in between the legs. The ritual was thorough, though no white man a-complaining of the smell of wogs knows anything about it. Then he dressed himself fastidiously. By this time he was ready to prepare breakfast.[5]

Breakfast! How he enjoyed taking in a tray of warm breakfast to his wife, cuddled in bed.[6] To appear there in his supremest immaculacy, tray in hand when his wife comes out of ether° to behold him. These things we blacks want to do for our own ... not fawningly for the whites for whom we bloody-well got to do it. He felt, he denied, that he was one of those who believed in putting his wife in her place even if she was a good wife. Not he.

◇ 'Solicitous' means that she shows great concern for her husband's welfare.

◇ Words such as 'ether', 'supremest immaculacy' and 'behold' have religious connotations.

5 The way Philemon washes himself is described as a 'ritual', a word which could have a religious meaning. It links to other words such as 'pure', ' Te Deum' and 'serenity'. What do these words suggest about Philemon's view of his wife and his marriage? What do the words 'thorough' and 'fastidiously' suggest about Philemon's character?

6 This shows us how Philemon would like his wife and others to see him.

CHARACTERIZATION

Matilda, too, appreciated her husband's kindness, and only put her foot down when he offered to wash up also.

'Off with you,' she scolded him on his way.[7]

At the bus-stop he was a little sorry to see that jovial old Maphikela was in a queue for a bus ahead of him. He would miss Maphikela's raucous laughter and uninhibited, bawdy conversations in fortissimo. Maphikela hailed him nevertheless. He thought he noticed hesitation in the old man, and a slight clouding of his countenance, but the old man shouted back at him, saying that he would wait for him at the terminus in town.[8]

Philemon considered this morning trip to town with garrulous° old Maphikela as his daily bulletin. All the township news was generously reported by loud-mouthed heralds, and spiritedly° discussed by the bus at large. Of course, 'news' included views on bosses (scurrilous), the Government (rude), Ghana and Russia (idolatrous), America and the West (sympathetically ridiculing), and boxing (bloodthirsty). But it was always stimulating and surprisingly comprehensive for so short a trip. And there was no law of libel.[9]

Maphikela was standing under one of those token bus-stop shelters that never keep out rain nor wind nor sun-heat. Philemon easily located him by his noisy ribbing of some office boys in their khaki-green uniforms. They walked together into town, but from Maphikela's suddenly subdued manner, Philemon

◇ 'Garrulous' means very talkative.

◇ 'Spiritedly' means enthusiastically.

7 What do these sentences reveal about the roles of men and women in the society that Philemon and Matilda live in? What do they suggest about Matilda's attitude to her husband and his duties?

8 Maphikela's face suddenly looks worried or sad. How does this statement prepare the reader for what he is going to tell Philemon?

9 The narrator seems to suggest that, despite any opinions to the contrary, township dwellers are knowledgeable, informed and interested in ideas and current events.

gathered that there was something serious coming up. Maybe a loan.

Eventually, Maphikela came out with it.

'Son,' he said sadly, 'if I could've avoided this, believe you me I would, but my wife is nagging the spice out of my life for not talking to you about it.'

It just did not become blustering old Maphikela to sound so grave and Philemon took compassion° upon him.

'Go ahead, dad,' he said generously. 'You know you can talk to me about anything.'

The old man gave a pathetic smile. 'We-e-e-ll, it's not really any of our business ... er ... but my wife felt ... you see. Damn it all! I wish these women would not snoop around so much.'[10] Then he rushed it. 'Anyway, it seems there's a young man who's going to visit your wife every morning ... ah ... for these last bloomin' three months. And that wife of mine swears by her heathen gods you don't know a thing about it.'

10 Why do you think Maphikela is reluctant to tell Philemon the news?

It was not quite like the explosion of a devastating bomb. It was more like the critical breakdown in an infinitely delicate piece of mechanism.[11] From outside the machine just seemed to have gone dead. But deep in its innermost recesses, menacing electrical flashes were leaping from coil to coil, and hot, viscous molten metal was creeping upon the fuel tanks ...

Philemon heard gears grinding and screaming in his head ...

'Dad,' he said hoarsely, 'I ... I have to go back home.'

He turned round and did not hear old

11 The 'infinitely delicate mechanism' seems to refer to the careful construction Philemon has built in his own head about the world around him and his role in it. In Philemon's mind he and his life are perfect. However, at the first hint of trouble, his life seems to be in danger of collapsing.

CHARACTERIZATION

Maphikela's anxious, 'Steady, son. Steady, son.'

The bus ride home was a torture of numb dread and suffocating despair. Though the bus was now emptier Philemon suffered crushing claustrophobia. There were immense washerwomen whose immense bundles of soiled laundry seemed to baulk and menace him. From those bundles crept miasmata◇ of sweaty intimacies that sent nauseous waves up and down from his viscera.◇ Then the wild swaying of the bus as it negotiated Mayfair Circle hurtled him sickeningly from side to side. Some of the younger women shrieked delightedly to the driver, '*Fuduga*! ... Stir the pot!' as he swung his steering-wheel this way and that. Normally, the crazy tilting of the bus gave him a prickling exhilaration. But now ...12

He felt like getting out of there, screamingly, elbowing everything out of his way. He wished this insane trip were over, and then again, he recoiled at the thought of getting home. He made a tremendous resolve to gather in all the torn, tingling threads of his nerves contorting in the raw. By a merciless act of will, he kept them in subjugation◇ as he stepped out of the bus back in the Victoria Road terminus, Sophiatown.13

The calm he achieved was tense ... but he could think now ... he could take a decision ...14

With almost boyishly innocent urgency, he rushed through his kitchen into his bedroom. In the lightning flash that the

◇ 'Miasmata' are unhealthy or unpleasant smells.

◇ This refers to the organs and cavities of the body; especially those in the abdomen.

◇ 'Subjugation' means defeat; to subjugate is to gain mastery or control over someone.

12 The descriptive words used here are an indication to the reader that something dangerous, 'menacing' or life-threatening is about to happen.

13 Look at how Philemon's entire character seems to have been reversed. Previously, the expression of unease on Maphikela's face filled Philemon with excessive concern or compassion. Now, however, he is described as 'merciless'. If Philemon's will is 'merciless', what do we expect of the way he might treat his wife?

14 This is how Philemon responds to the anxiety he

eye can whip, he saw it all ... the man beside his wife ... the chestnut arm around her neck ... the ruffled candlewick bedspread ... the suit across the chair. But he affected not to see.[15]

He opened the wardrobe door, and as he dug into it, he cheerfully spoke to his wife, 'Fancy, Tilly, I forgot to take my pass. I had already reached town and was going to walk up to the office. If it hadn't been for wonderful old Mr Maphikela.'

A swooshing noise of violent retreat and the clap of his bedroom window stopped him. He came from behind the wardrobe door and looked out from the open window. A man clad only in vest and underpants was running down the street. Slowly he turned around and contemplated ... the suit.

Philemon lifted it gingerly under his arm and looked a the stark horror in Matilda's eyes. She was now sitting up in bed. Her mouth twitched, but her throat raised no words.[16]

'Ha,' he said, 'I see we have a visitor,' indicating the blue suit. 'We really must show some of our hospitality. But first, I must phone my boss that I can't come to work today ... mmmm-er, my wife's not well. Be back in a moment, then we can make arrangements.'

He took the suit along.[17]

When he returned he found Matilda weeping on the bed. He dropped the suit beside her, pulled up the chair, turned it round so that its back came in front of him, sat down, brought his chin onto his folded arms before him, and waited for her.

experiences. This reaction seems prophetic of his treatment of Matilda. Notice that Philemon has not thought of Matilda even once. He is only concerned with his own anger.

15 In one glance Philemon sees exactly what is going on: Matilda is in bed with another man, whose suit is draped over the chair. But he pretends not to have seen it. Can you think of other things Philemon chose to ignore in the past?

16 If Philemon has always been merciful and good to his wife (as he believes he has), then why is she so terrified of him now?

17 Why do you think Philemon focuses on the suit and not on Matilda?

CHARACTERIZATION

◇ Something 'inscrutable' is impossible to understand.

After a while the convulsions of her shoulders ceased. She saw a smug man with an odd smile and meaningless inscrutability◇ in his eyes. He spoke to her with very little noticeable emotion; if anything, with a flutter of humour.18

'We have a visitor, Tilly.' His mouth curved ever so slightly. 'I'd like him to be treated with the greatest of consideration. He will eat every meal with us and share all we have. Since we have no spare room, he'd better sleep in here. But the point is, Tilly that you will meticulously look after him. If he vanishes or anything else happens to him ...' A shaft of evil shot from his eye ...   'Matilda, I'll kill you.'

He rose from the chair and looked with incongruous supplication at her. He told her to put the fellow in the wardrobe for the time being. As she passed him to get the suit, he turned to go. She ducked frantically, and he stopped.19

'You don't seem to understand me, Matilda. There's to be no violence in this house if you and I can help it. So just look after that suit.' He went out.20

He went out to the Sophiatown Post Office, which is placed on the exact line between Sophiatown and the white man's surly Westdene. He posted his boss's letters, and walked to the beerhall at the tail end of Western Native Township. He had never been inside it before, but somehow the thunderous din laved his bruised spirit. He stayed there all day.

He returned home for supper ... and surprise. His dingy little home had been transformed, and the air of stern mas-

18 For the first time we glimpse the world from Matilda's perspective. The Philemon that Matilda sees is not the Philemon we have 'seen' riding on the bus. Matilda does not see that Philemon is upset, but rather that he is unfeeling about what has happened and even feels pleased with himself and amused by the situation. Do you think that, perhaps in the past too, Philemon's responses to his wife seemed 'inscrutable' to her?

19 She ducks because she expects him to beat her.

20 Consider Philemon's behaviour from Matilda's perspective. Why does he focus on the suit and not on the fact that he has caught her being unfaithful? Note the threatening tone of his voice and content of his words. Is this the same Philemon we saw in the first part of the story? What made his character change?

◇ 'Stern masculinity' implies that the house was 'cruel, strict and uncompromising' even before Matilda's unfaithfulness was detected.

◇ The use of words and phrases such as 'gripped', 'overwhelming, undisciplined force', 'catapult', and 'glowed fiercely' emphasize the power of this force.

◇ 'Dexterous' means that she worked in an efficient way.

culinity◇ it had hitherto contained had been wiped away, to be replaced by anxious feminine touches here and there.[21] There were even gay, colourful curtains swirling in the kitchen window. The old-fashioned coal-stove gleamed in its blackness. A clean, chequered oil cloth on the table. Supper ready.

Then she appeared in the doorway of the bedroom.[22] Heavens! Here was the woman he had married; the young, fresh, cocoa-coloured maid who had sent rushes of emotion shuddering through him. And the dress she wore brought out all the girlishness of her, hidden so long beneath German print. But no hint of coquettishness, although she stood in the doorway and slid her arm up the jamb, and shyly slanted her head to the other shoulder. She smiled weakly.

What makes a woman like this experiment with adultery? He wondered.

Philemon closed his eyes and gripped◇ the seat of his chair on both sides as some overwhelming, undisciplined force sought to catapult him towards her. For a moment some essence glowed fiercely within him, then sank back into itself and died ... [23]

He sighed and smiled sadly back at her, 'I'm hungry, Tilly.'

The spell snapped, and she was galvanized into action. She prepared his supper with dexterous◇ hands that trembled a little only when they hesitated in mid-air. She took her seat opposite him, regarded him curiously, clasped her hands waiting for his prayer, but in her heart she mur-

21 Does this description suggest anything about their relationship?

22 Matilda tries to calm down her husband's anger by being even more submissive to him than she has been before. She tries to make things beautiful, but her efforts are those of a woman who is very scared ('anxious'). Why has Matilda's femininity been hidden so long?

23 For the first time Philemon looks at his wife and considers her motives. What is this 'overwhelming, undisciplined force', this 'essence that glowed' in him, and that makes him want to be close to her? Is this essence love? Is it sexual desire? What does the death of this essence imply about the basis of his behaviour towards Matilda in the rest of the story?

CHARACTERIZATION

mured some other, much more urgent prayer of her own.[24]

'Matilda!' he barked. 'Our visitor!' The sheer savagery with which he cracked at her jerked her up, but only when she saw the brute cruelty in his face did she run out of the room, toppling the chair behind her.[25]

She returned with the suit on a hanger, and stood there quivering like a feather. She looked at him with helpless dismay. The demonical rage in his face was evaporating, but his heavy breathing still rocked his thorax above the table, to and fro.

'Put a chair, there.' He indicated with a languid gesture of his arm. She moved like a ghost as she drew a chair to the table.

'Now seat our friend at the table ... no, no, not like that. Put him in front of the chair, and place him on the seat so that he becomes indeed the third person.'

Philemon went on relentlessly: 'Dish up for him. Generously. I imagine he hasn't had a morsel all day, the poor devil.'[26]

She served the suit. The act was so ridiculous that she carried it out with a bitter sense of humiliation. He came back to sit down and plunge into his meal. No grace was said for the first time in this house. With his mouth full, he indicated by a toss of his head that she should sit down in her place. She did so. Glancing at her plate, the thought occurred to her that someone, after a long famine, was served a sumptuous supper, but as the food reached her mouth it

24 Which words reveal that Matilda is feeling very anxious?

25 Words like 'bark', 'savagery' and 'cruelty' are all associated with cruel and inhuman behaviour. Words like 'quivering' and 'dismay' describe Matilda's fear and helplessness. Compare these words to those used to describe Philemon.

26 Philemon has no mercy and is enjoying his wife's humiliation. Do you think Philemon behaves in an appropriate way?

turned to sawdust. Where had she heard it? [27]

Matilda could not eat. She suddenly broke into tears.

Philemon took no notice of her weeping. After supper, he casually gathered the dishes and started washing up. He flung a dry cloth at her without saying a word. She rose and went to stand by his side drying up. But for their wordlessness, they seemed a very devoted couple. [28]

After washing up, he took the suit and turned to her. 'That's how I want it every meal, every day.' Then he walked into the bedroom. [29]

So it was. After that first breakdown, Matilda began to feel that her punishment was not too severe, considering the heinousness of the crime. She tried to put a joke into it, but by slow, unconscious degrees, the strain nibbled at her. Philemon did not harass her much more, so long as the ritual with the confounded suit was conscientiously followed. [30]

Only once, he got one of his malevolent brainwaves. He got it into his head that 'our visitor' needed an outing. Accordingly the suit was taken to the dry-cleaners during the week, and, come Sunday, they had to take it out for a walk. Both Philemon and Matilda dressed for the occasion. Matilda had to carry the suit on its hanger over her back and the three of them strolled leisurely along Ray Street. They passed the church crowd in front of the famous Anglican Mission of Christ the King. Though the worshippers

27 Think of the pure, almost religious way in which Philemon saw himself at the beginning of the story. Does this behaviour, motivated by 'demonical rage', concur with how he saw himself?

28 The word 'seemed' is a key word here. Formerly they also appeared happy, but were they really?

29 Note how Philemon rules Matilda.

30 Matilda is completely submissive and begins to think that her punishment suits the wickedness ('heinousness') of her mistake. But is her punishment suited to her crime? Even though she does not admit it, the daily tension of the ritual with the suit affects her nerves. She thinks that he does not 'harass' her much, but the continuous emotional harassment is evident.

CHARACTERIZATION

saw nothing unusual in them, Matilda felt, searing through her, red-hot needles of embarrassment, and every needle-point was a public eye piercing into her degradation.[31]

But Philemon walked casually on. He led her down Ray Street and turned into Main Road. He stopped often to look into shop windows or to greet a friend passing by. They went up Toby Street, turned into Edward Road, and back home. To Philemon the outing was free of incident, but to Matilda it was one long, excruciating incident.

At home, he grabbed a book on ab-normal psychology, flung himself into a chair and calmly said to her, 'Give the old chap a rest, will you, Tilly?'[32]

In the bedroom, Matilda said to herself that things could not go on like this. She thought of how she could bring the matter to a head with Philemon; have it out with him for once and for all. But the memory of his face, that first day she had forgotten to entertain the suit, stayed her. She thought of running away, but where to? Home? What could she tell her old-fashioned mother had happened between Philemon and her? All right, run away clean then. She thought of many young married girls who were divorcees now, who had won their freedom.[33]

What had happened to Staff Nurse Kakile? The woman drank heavily now, and when she got drunk, the boys of Sophiatown passed her around and called her the Cesspot.

Matilda shuddered.

31 Matilda's humiliation becomes public here. If you are familiar with the biblical story of the crucifixion, does this scene remind you of Christ carrying his cross pub-licly? Matilda is still paying for her 'sin', for which her husband never forgives her.

32 Do you think the nature of his reading material is significant? Why? Philemon refers to the suit in terms that appear to be friendly, such as 'the old chap' and 'our friend'. However, he is sarcastic and takes every opportunity to remind Matilda of her unfaithfulness.

33 We get a glimpse here of Matilda's feelings. She is reaching the end of her tether. Her first desire is to resolve the issue with Phil-emon, but she fears his rage. The society in which she lives sees men as superior to women. Although Matilda

An idea struck her. There were still decent, married women around Sophiatown.[34] She remembered how after the private schools had been forced to close with the advent of Bantu Education, Father Harringway of the Anglican Mission had organized Cultural Clubs.[35] One, she seemed to remember, was for married women. If only she could lose herself in some cultural activity, find absolution for her conscience in some doing good; that would blur her blasted home life, would restore her self-respect. After all, Philemon had not broadcast her disgrace abroad ... nobody knew; not one of Sophiatown's slander-mongers suspected how vulnerable she was. She must go and see Mrs Montjane about joining a Cultural Club. She must ask Philemon now if she might ... she must ask him nicely.[36]

She got up and walked into the other room where Philemon was reading quietly. She dreaded disturbing him, did not know how to begin talking to him ... they had talked so little for so long. She went and stood in front of him, looking silently upon his deep concentration. Presently, he looked up with a frown on his face. [37]

Then she dared, 'Phil, I'd like to join one of those Cultural Clubs for married women. Would you mind?'

He wrinkled his nose and rubbed it between thumb and index finger as he considered the request. But he had caught the note of anxiety of in her voice and thought he knew what it meant.

would like to be free of this oppressive marriage, she does not have the courage to confront Philemon or to leave him. Do you think this is the best thing for Matilda to do?

34 Does Matilda see herself as one of the 'decent, married women', or has she come to see herself as Philemon sees her?

35 The reader is reminded of the background against which the story is set.

36 Matilda does not have the courage to confront Philemon, so she hopes to 'lose herself' — to forget about her terrible situation by doing something good and having contact with other people.

37 Do you think they used to talk more before Matilda's unfaithfulness was discovered?

'Mmmm,' he said, nodding. 'I think that's a good idea. You can't be moping around here all day. Yes, you may, Tilly.' Then he returned to his book.[38]

The Cultural Club idea was wonderful. She found women like herself, with time (if not with tragedy) on their hands, engaged in wholesome, refreshing activities.[39] The atmosphere was cheerful and cathartic. They learned things and they did things. They organized fêtes, bazaars, youth activities, sport, music, self-help and community projects. She got involved in committees, meetings, debates, conferences. It was for her a whole new venture into humancraft, and her personality blossomed. Philemon gave her all the rein she wanted.[40]

Now, abiding by that silly ritual at home seemed a little thing ... a very little thing ...[41]

Then one day she decided to organize a little party for her friends and their husbands. Philemon was very decent about it. He said it was all right. He even gave her extra money for it. Of course, she knew nothing of the strain he himself suffered from his mode of castigation.[42]

There was a week of hectic preparation. Philemon stepped out of its cluttering way as best he could. So many things seemed to be taking place simultaneously. New dresses were made. Cakes were baked; three different orders of meat prepared; beef for the uninvited chancers; mutton for the normal guests; turkey and chicken for the inner pith of the club's core. To Philemon, it looked as if

38 Philemon exploits her fear. Why do you think he allows her to participate in the activities of the women's club?

39 This suggests that there might be other women with similar problems to hers. For the first time, Matilda has an opportunity for personal growth.

40 This sentence has an ominous tone. Philemon will allow Matilda freedom ('gave her rein'), but only for a short while before he will 'rein her in' again.

41 Matilda tries to persuade herself that her fate is not as bad as it seems.

42 Does this suggest that the way in which Philemon treats Matilda might be having an impact on him too?

Matilda planned to feed the multitude on the Mount with no aid of miracles.[43]

On the Sunday of the party, Philemon saw Matilda's guests. He was surprised by the handsome grace with which she received them. There was a long table with enticing foods and flowers and serviettes. Matilda placed all her guests round the table, and the party was ready to begin in the mock-formal township fashion. Outside a steady rumble of conversation went on where the human odds and ends of every Sophiatown party had their 'share'.[44]

Matilda caught a curious look on Philemon's face. He tried to disguise his edict◇ when he said, 'Er – the guest of honour.'[45]

But Matilda took a chance. She begged, 'Just this once, Phil.'

He became livid. 'Matilda!' he shouted. 'Get our visitor!' Then with incisive sarcasm, 'Or are you ashamed of him?'[46]

She went ash-grey; but there was nothing for it but to fetch her albatross.[47] She came back and squeezed a chair into some corner, and placed the suit on it. Then slowly she placed a plate of food before it. For a while the guests were dumbfounded. Then curiosity flooded in. They talked at the same time. 'What's the idea, Philemon?'...'Why must she serve a suit?' ... 'What's happening?' Some just giggled in a silly way. Philemon carelessly swung his head towards Matilda. 'You better ask my wife. She knows the fellow best.'

All interest beamed upon poor

◇ An 'edict' is an official statement issued by an authority. The word reveals the power Philemon wields.

43 More religious imagery that seems to suggest that things are improving for Matilda. The biblical reference is to Jesus' feeding more than 5000 people by miraculously multiplying five loaves of bread and two fishes.

44 Matilda has grown and regained some of her self-respect.

45 Again, Philemon is amused and delights in his wife's humiliation.

46 Philemon exploits the situation to the full and wields all the power he has over her to humiliate her in front of the guests.

47 An albatross is a large sea bird. People believe that killing an albatross brings bad luck, even death. Matilda's albatross, then, is something which causes her much discomfort and difficulty.

Matilda. For a moment she could not speak, all enveloped in misery. Then she said, unconvincingly, 'It's just a game that my husband and I play at mealtime.' They roared with laughter. Philemon let her get away with it.[48]

The party went on, and every time Philemon's glare sent Matilda scurrying to serve the suit each course; the guests were no-end amused by the persistent mock-seriousness with which husband and wife played out their little game. Only, to Matilda, it was no joke; it was a hot poker◇ down her throat. After the party, Philemon went off with one of the guests who promised to show him a joint 'that sells genuine stuff, boy, genuine stuff.'

Reeling drunk, late that sabbath, he crashed through his kitchen door, towards his bedroom.[49] Then he saw her.

They have a way of saying in the argot◇ of Sophiatown, 'Cook out of the head!' signifying that someone was impacted with such violent shock that whatever whiffs of alcohol still wandered through his head were instantaneously evaporated and the man stood sober before stark reality.[50]

There she lay, curled as if just before she died she begged for a little love, implored some implacable lover to cuddle her a little ... just this once ... just this once more.[51]

In screwish anguish,◇ Philemon cried, 'Tilly!'

◇ A 'hot poker' is a red-hot metal bar.

◇ Argot is language specific to one group of people.

◇ 'Screwish anguish' conjures up an image of extreme torture and pain.

48 The guests do not realize that the situation is serious; there is no game involved, but a malicious ritual.

49 He has tried to escape by drinking alcohol.

50 At what other times in this story has he faced reality?

51 Even in her death she is begging for love. Did she receive such love from Philemon? Why did she have an affair? 'Implacable' means that the 'lover' could never be satisfied or changed. Who is this lover?

2 Investigating the text

'The Suit' is a challenging story that raises difficult questions about human behaviour and relationships. Who are these characters and why do they behave in the ways they do? Is Philemon's treatment of Matilda fair or not? Is he justified in punishing her for being unfaithful to him? Why does Matilda kill herself? Can we hold Philemon responsible for her death?

Before we can offer an informed opinion on these or any other questions about the story, we need to have a very clear grasp of what happens in it and of the characters involved.

Fortunately, we can develop skills to help us read and understand texts. Like police detectives who might investigate the facts surrounding Matilda's death, we need to become literary detectives who have to sift through the layers of evidence provided in the text. The rest of this section outlines some of the strategies we can adopt to enhance our understanding of literary texts.

LOOKING FOR CLUES: THE PLOT

At the beginning of our literary detective work, we need to find out what happens in the story under investigation. The literary term for the series of events (or happenings) in a story is the plot. Plot is important, because our knowledge of what happens will influence the way we see characters and the motives for their behaviour.

You can use a time line to map or summarize the plot of a story. A good understanding of the sequence of events allows us to see how they are linked and to decide on the causes and effects of specific actions and attitudes.

LOOKING FOR CLUES: THE CONTEXT

The events in a story always occur in a particular context. Context, as we said earlier in this chapter, refers to the set of circumstances in which something takes place. Context includes the place where and the time when events occur. If we can understand the background against which things happen, we have better insight into the events and the characters, and ultimately the meaning of the story. As literary detectives we would ask:

✪ What is the relationship between the context and the motives and the actions of characters?

✪ To what extent have the realities of a particular time and place influenced the actions shown in the text?

The events in 'The Suit' take place in Sophiatown before black people were removed by the National Party government. The narrator's description of Philemon's surroundings gives us clues about living conditions in Sophiatown at this time:

> From behind the kitchen door, he removed an old rain cape peeling off in places, and swung it over his head. He dashed for the lavatory, nearly slipping in a pool of muddy water, but he reached the door. Aw, blast, someone had made it before him. Well, that is the toll of staying in a yard where twenty ... thirty other people have to share the same lean-to. He was dancing and burning in that climactic moment when the trouser-fly will not come wide soon enough.

Poverty, over-crowding and inadequate facilities typify the environment in which Philemon and Matilda live. We need to ask whether these difficult conditions have had any impact on these characters and their behaviour. Is there any suggestion that they act as they do because of their living conditions? Or is the behaviour of the characters in contrast to what we, the readers, might expect given the circumstances? In most instances, we would not expect to find a direct, uncomplicated relationship between context and character. Nevertheless, we need to assess the extent to which circumstances help to explain the characters and their actions.

LOOKING FOR CLUES: MEETING THE CHARACTERS

Philemon and Matilda are the central characters in 'The Suit'. Neither character is fixed or static in behaviour or personality. As we read through the story our impression of these characters changes as we see them in different situations.

We might see Philemon in at least five ways as we read through the story, as a:
- a devoted husband,
- a hard-working man and a good friend,
- a cold, authoritarian and vengeful husband,
- a cruel man who takes pleasure in humiliating others, and
- a remorseful person in pain.

Each of these different ways of seeing Philemon occurs as our perspective alters according to his actions, particularly in the face of crisis. Together, these different perspectives provide the reader with an integrated picture of his character. As we know, all people have different facets to their personalities. Someone might be both strict and compassionate, patient in one situation and irritable in another, or loving in some contexts and cruel in others. These different facets of character combine to form a unique identity. As we read 'The Suit' we continually adjust our idea of Philemon's identity (and the identities of the other characters).

In the case of Philemon, readers realize that the picture that they have formed of him early on in the story might not be an entirely accurate or complete view of his character. Certain aspects of his personality are concealed or are only hinted at indirectly.

What does this description of Philemon suggest about him and about his relationship with Matilda?

> He had a trick for these morning chores. When the fire in the old stove warmed up, the water kettle humming on it, he gathered and laid ready the things he would need for the day: briefcase and the files that go with it; the book that he was reading currently; the letters of his lawyer boss which he usually posted before he reached the office; his wife's and his own dry-cleaning slips for the Sixty-Minutes; his lunch tin solicitously prepared the night before by his attentive wife; and, today, the battered rain cape. By the time the kettle on the stove sang (before it actually boiled), he poured water from it into a washbasin, refilled and replaced it on the stove. Then he washed himself carefully: across the eyes, under, in and out the armpits, down the torso and in between the legs. The ritual was thorough, though no white man a-complaining of the smell of wogs knows anything about it. Then he dressed himself fastidiously. By this time he was ready to prepare breakfast.
>
> Breakfast! How he enjoyed taking in a tray of warm breakfast to his wife, cuddled in bed. To appear there in his supremest immaculacy, tray in hand when his wife comes out of ether to behold him.

Philemon sees himself as a devoted husband and his wife as a 'serene' and 'pure' woman. However, the moment he discovers that Matilda has flaws, his personality seems to change. In stories, as in life, it is often in times of crisis that a person is most likely to reveal hidden aspects of their character. At the first hint of trouble, Philemon exposes a side to his character that is not evident from the opening descriptions of a contented married man in a happy domestic environment. The internal tensions within Philemon's personality – the contrast between his idealistic view of life and his inner insecurity – are revealed by Philemon's reaction to Maphikela's information that Matilda is being visited by a strange man. To refresh your memory, reread the section of 'The Suit' where Philemon and Maphikela meet in the bus queue.

Philemon's immediate, devastating suspicion is in conflict with his thoughts and ideas at the beginning of the story. Would a loving, trusting husband who believes in the purity of his wife be swayed by an unproven suggestion of her unfaithfulness? It seems as though Philemon's notion that their lives are perfect clashes with the way he actually behaves when his beliefs are put to the test. In crisis Philemon's character crumbles; it falls apart. We have two different character portrayals of Philemon now: Philemon as he appears at the beginning of the story, and Philemon as he responds to Maphikela's news.

✪ Do you think Philemon has a realistic idea of what his wife is like? Do you think Matilda can live up to Philemon's expect-ations of her as a perfect wife?

✪ How does the image of Philemon conveyed in the passage above contrast with his behaviour towards Matilda later in the story?

✪ Does his treatment of Matilda after he has discovered her unfaithfulness mean that Philemon is actually an incredibly cruel and vindictive character?

✪ Consider Philemon's response when he discovers his wife's body. Is this the response of a cruel and vindictive man?

Now that we have considered Philemon as a character we need to look at Matilda and how she sees the world. We also need to think about how she is seen by other people. At this point, you need to go back to the personality quiz in chapter one.

✪ Imagine that you are Matilda. What answers do you think Matilda would give to the questions in the personality quiz?

✪ Do you think Matilda's answers would be the same through-out the story?

Copy and complete the following table to compare perspectives on Matilda before and after her unfaithfulness is discovered.

	Matilda's view of herself	Philemon's view of Matilda
Before her unfaithfulness is discovered		
After her unfaithfulness has been discovered		
Before she joins the Cultural Club		
After she joins the Cultural Club		

Matilda's character changes over the course of the events depicted in the story. Immediately after Philemon has caught her in bed with another man, Matilda tries to please her husband by making their house and herself beautiful:

> He returned home for supper ... and surprise. His dingy little home had been transformed, and the air of stern masculinity it had hitherto contained had been wiped away, to be replaced by anxious feminine touches here and there. There were even gay, colourful curtains swirling in the kitchen window. The old-fashioned coal-stove gleamed in its blackness. A clean, chequered oil cloth on the table. Supper ready.

✪ Have you ever tried especially hard to please someone because they were very angry with you? What did you do? Why did you behave in this way?
✪ Why do you think Matilda wants to please Philemon? What clues does this give us about how she feels about herself?

We suspect that Matilda has a low sense of self-esteem. She does not think highly of herself. The text of the story also tells us that she is afraid of what might happen to her should she have to survive on her own, without a husband. When Matilda joins the Cultural Club her attitude towards herself begins to change. She slowly discovers a new sense of self-worth. It is partly as a result of these changes that Matilda's death by suicide is so shocking.

CHARACTER AND MEANING

An understanding of the relationship between character and events (plot) can help us understand the hidden motives and reasons for the behaviour of the people we meet in life and in stories. Can Themba's short story raises many pertinent questions about character and behaviour. What we think about the issues it raises will depend both on how well we have understood the story, and on the attitudes that we bring to bear on its events. Some of these attitudes, particularly those concerned with women and race, are explored later in this book. For the meantime, we need to be aware that any response to a literary text is complex.

TIME OFF
TO THINK!

- Why is Matilda unfaithful to her husband?
- How does one expect Philemon to behave when he discovers that his wife has been unfaithful?
- How does Philemon actually respond to the discovery of his wife in bed with her lover? Does he respond in the way one would expect?
- Is Philemon's response to his wife's infidelity appropriate? Can you think of other ways in which he could have responded that might have been better for both of them?
- Is Philemon justified in choosing to continue punishing his wife in the way he does, long after she has been unfaithful?
- Is there any specific point at which Philemon should have forgiven her?

THE NARRATOR

In our earlier discussion of first-person and third-person narrators, we made the point that narrative perspective influences readers to sympathize with certain characters more than others. In 'The Suit' the narrative voice leads the reader into seeing the characters in particular ways. For example, when we finish reading 'The Suit', we might be appalled by Philemon's behaviour, and we might be horrified by the consequences of his actions. However, most readers are also, probably, left with some sympathy for him. Why does this happen? What is it that makes our reactions to Philemon so complicated and even contradictory?

One important influence on us is the narrator's technique of concentrating on Philemon's emotions and point of view at important stages in the story. Think about the end of the story in particular – his emotions are described in forceful and unusual terms ('In screwish anguish, Philemon cried, "Tilly!"'). Even though we might feel that Philemon is to blame for Matilda's suicide, the narrator tells us that he suffers terrible emotional pain because of her death. Since we as readers might also feel upset by the story, and especially by Matilda's suicide, there is a sense in which we are led by this to identify with Philemon. In sharing similar reactions with him we also share a similar point of view (or perspective) on the suicide. At least to some extent, we see things the way he sees them.

. . . .

IN CHAPTER ONE WE SAID that successful writing was more than simply listing events, and that as writers we need to take care to interest our readers. In this section, we will explore some methods of writing about people descriptively. Descriptive writing creates interest because it allows readers to visualize more vividly the scene, event or person being described.

FOUR

DESCRIBING PEOPLE

1 Descriptive words: adjectives and adverbs

Here is an example of descriptive writing from the opening chapter of the novel *Snow Falling on Cedars* by David Guterson.

HE ACCUSED MAN, Kabuo Miyamoto, sat proudly upright with a rigid grace, his palms placed softly on the defendant's table – the posture of a man who has detached himself insofar as this is possible at his own trial. Some in the gallery would later say that his stillness suggested a disdain for the proceedings; others felt certain it veiled a fear of the verdict that was to come. Whichever it was, Kabuo showed nothing – not even a flicker of the eyes. He was dressed in a white shirt worn buttoned to the throat and gray, neatly pressed trousers. His figure, especially the neck and shoulders, communicated the impression of irrefutable physical strength and of precise, even imperial bearing. Kabuo's features were smooth and angular; his hair had been cropped close to his skull in a manner that made its musculature prominent. In the face of the charge that had been leveled against him he sat with his dark eyes trained straight ahead and did not appear moved at all. ...

Snow fell that morning outside the courthouse windows, four tall, narrow arches of leaded glass that yielded a great quantity of weak December light. A wind from the sea lofted snowflakes against the windowpanes, where they melted and ran toward the casements. Beyond the courthouse the town of Amity Harbour spread along the island shoreline. A few wind-whipped and decrepit Victorian mansions, remnants of a lost era of seagoing optimism, loomed out of the snowfall on the town's sporadic hills. Beyond them, cedars wove a steep mat of still green. The snow blurred from vision the clean contours of these cedar hills. The sea wind drove snowflakes steadily inland, hurling them against the fragrant trees, and the snow began to settle on the highest branches with a gentle implacability.

The accused man, with one segment of his consciousness, watched the falling snow outside the windows. He had been exiled in the county jail for seventy-seven days – the last part of September, all of October and all of November, the first week of December in jail. There was no window anywhere in his basement cell, no portal through which the autumn light could come to him. He had missed autumn, he realized now – it had passed already, evaporated. The snowfall, which he witnessed out of the corners of his eyes – furious, wind-whipped flakes against the windows – struck him as infinitely beautiful.

FROM: David Guterson, *Snow Falling on Cedars*, pp. 3–5. 1995. New York and Toronto: Vintage Contemporaries (Random House).

In this extract the character, Kabuo Miyamoto, is introduced as 'the accused man', but this representation of him is then expanded and modified by the other ways in which he is described. Details are given about how he sits, what he looks like, and the expression on his face. These details also reveal a sense of what he feels and thinks without directly stating his thoughts and feelings. This is added to by the descriptions of his surroundings, because his response to things such as the snowfall suggest even more about his character. His thoughts about the snowfall and the passing of time show us aspects of his sadness and frustration. He focuses on the loss or 'evaporation' of autumn, a time that he could not experience fully as he was in jail, and the appearance of snowflakes being driven violently by the wind seems to reflect his own sense of being trapped but angry. Make a list of the words and phrases in the extract which you find particularly descriptive of Kabuo Miyamoto's appearance and character. Most of the words that describe Kabuo Miyamoto fall into the grammatical category of adjectives. Adjectives are commonly found in descriptions of people, places and objects. They modify nouns or pronouns. Descriptive words can also be adverbs. These are words that give more detail and information about verbs: where, when and how actions occur.

ADJECTIVES AND ADVERBS

ADJECTIVES

Adjectives are words that modify or describe nouns, making them more specific and more detailed.

In English, adjectives can be used in different places in a sentence:
- ✪ before nouns, as in 'A colourful flag'
- ✪ after linking verbs such as 'be', 'seem' and 'look'; for example, 'you look elegant' and 'She is clever'
- ✪ after pronouns ending in '-body', '-one', '-thing' and '-where'; for example, 'somewhere quiet', or 'something entertaining'.

> Adjectives and adverbs can be graded to indicate their intensity. They can also be compared. The most common intensifier is 'very', as in 'He is very angry'. There are three degrees of comparison: for instance, 'cold', 'colder', 'coldest'; 'good', 'better', 'best'.

ADVERBS

Adverbs are words that modify or describe verbs. Adverbs answer the questions 'how?', 'when?' and 'where?' about verbs.

We can use adverbs for different purposes:
- ✪ adverbs can describe verbs in greater detail; for example, 'she smiles cheerfully'
- ✪ we can use adverbs for emphasis, for example, 'He has definitely committed the crime'
- ✪ adverbs can also modify adjectives; for example, 'I am extremely confused'
- ✪ adverbs can modify whole sentences, for example 'Unfortunately, you have arrived too late for the examination'.

Now try using adjectives and adverbs to describe someone. You need not describe an invented character; it may be someone you know.
- ✪ Choose no more than six adjectives that you think characterize the person. Some of your adjectives should describe the person's appearance and some should describe his or her personality. Think of how they dress and what they look like. What is their voice like? Do they have any peculiar characteristics that set them aside from other people?

✪ Now choose adverbs to describe this person's actions.

✪ Use these adjectives and adverbs to help you write a paragraph about the person you have chosen to describe. Try to convey to your reader a clear picture of what they are like and how they behave.

 ## Describing other people: actions

Authors do not create characters only by using adjectives. Fantasy author Terry Pratchett, for instance, says that one should not 'describe' fictional characters: one should, instead, allow their personalities to emerge from what they do and say. This idea is based on the assumption that a character will speak and behave in a certain way, in accordance with his or her nature. Of course, the author still has to create and visualize that character, but the idea is that the author also uses actions to characterize the person. Certainly we gain most of our insight into the people we know from what they say and do, not only from what they look like.

Try to capture someone's character by recording a conversation:

> **FLESHING MY CHARACTERS**
> Deborah Moggach
>
> Once a character has gelled it's an unmistakable sensation, like an engine starting up within one's body. From then onwards, one is driven by this other person, seeing things through their eyes, shuffling around the shops as a 57-year-old divorced man and practically feeling one has grown a beard.
>
> FROM: Clare Boylan (ed.)
> *The Agony and the Ego: the art and strategy of fiction writing explored.*
> 1993. London: Penguin.

✪ Think of an interesting person you know. Perhaps this will be someone who has had an unusual experience or who is very old.

✪ Take a tape recorder and interview this person. Ask them questions about their life and experiences.

✪ Set aside time to transcribe (write down) exactly what was said in the interview. (Your writer's journal would be a good place to do this.)

WHAT YOU SHOULD end up with is a dialogue that looks something like the discussion between Larry and J. B. in chapter one (page 19).

✪ Does your transcription capture the personality or character of the person you interviewed?

✪ Add words or phrases to your dialogue that describe exactly how the person being interviewed behaved and reacted.

HINTS

● IT HELPS to prepare your questions in advance.

● MAKE notes during the interview. These will refresh your memory when you transcribe the conversation afterwards.

● DON'T TRY to write down the entire interview. Choose the most interesting part of it and transcribe that.

Conveying someone's character in a life-like manner is challenging. Words often do not say exactly what we would like them to say. It is hard to find exactly the right expressions to indicate changes in the tone of a voice or shifts in facial expression. Your descriptive writing is more likely to be successful if you have observed your subject closely and selected those details which are most important or revealing. More importantly, you will have to spend time thinking about your choice of descriptive words and editing your original transcript.

Writing is a process. Even the most experienced writers write more than one draft of something. They go through a process of drafting, revising and rewriting until they are happy with the finished product. This is true both when you are writing an assignment essay and when you write a creative piece such as a poem or short story. When you write, you should follow these steps:

1 Carefully examine the topic on which you are to write; focus on what the topic requires you to write about.

2 Generate ideas about the topic. This is the planning stage of writing. Just write down ideas as they come to mind. Don't worry about putting your ideas down in a grammatical or well-phrased way at this stage. You could simply list ideas, make a mind-map or write down key words.

3 Now you are ready to write the first draft. Select the best ideas from the planning stage, put them together in sentences and organize these sentences into paragraphs.

4 The next stage is revision. Read through your first draft. Is your message clear? Is your writing interesting? Did you include all the relevant details?

5 Write the second draft, incorporating the improvements on your first draft. Now check the grammatical correctness of your piece of writing. Did you write full sentences? Have you used the correct tenses? Have you used punctuation marks correctly? Is your spelling correct?

CHARACTERIZATION

6 Finally, revise your writing until you are satisfied with it. Be sure to write an effective concluding paragraph to bring the piece of writing to a close. Ask someone you know (and trust) to read through what you have written and to comment on it.

To end this chapter, we are going to put these steps into practice. Listen to your taped interview again and read over your transcript. Using the steps above, write a description of the person you interviewed. Your description could take any form you like: a paragraph or two, a poem, a story, a letter to someone or an article for a magazine. Finally, show your work to other people who know that person and ask them what they think of it.

3 Made for Each Other: Ideas about Gender

THE PREVIOUS CHAPTERS looked at how we represent ourselves and other people. In this chapter we will explore ideas
about gender and think about the relationship between texts and
gender. As you work through this chapter, aim to spend time
developing your own understanding of some of the issues of
gender and representation.

The ideas and exercises in this chapter will help you to understand what the term gender refers to. They will also require you
to think about stereotypes and assumptions that relate to gender
issues. Since this chapter is designed as an introduction to thinking about gender in relation to writing and culture, we have
decided to concentrate on a limited number of relevant issues.
This chapter mostly focuses on ideas about gender in relation to
women. Historically, thinkers who have written and theorized
about gender have largely focused on ideas about women and
women's experiences. In many cases, such theorizing has
occurred in response to different forms of discrimination experienced by women in various cultures and societies. However, we
do not want to give the impression that ideas about gender only
apply to women, since the ways in which people think and write
about gender apply to all human beings. This chapter is a start-
ing-place for thinking about gender.

ONE

① What is gender?

> **gender** /ˈdʒendə(r)/ *n* [C, U] **1** (*grammar*) (in certain languages) the CLASSIFICATION(1) of nouns, adjectives or pronouns as MASCULINE(2), FEMININE(2) or NEUTER(1): *In French the adjective must agree with the noun in number and gender.* **2** the condition of being male or female: *gender issues.*

The word 'gender' has different uses depending on the context in which it appears. Firstly, it refers to the practice followed in certain languages of thinking of some words as 'masculine', some words as 'feminine' and other words as 'neuter' (not masculine or feminine). This does not mean that words which relate to women are classified as feminine or that words relating to men are described as masculine. Rather, it means there is a practice of organizing some languages using 'masculine', 'feminine' and 'neuter' as labels for words that share some specific similarities.

The similarities have nothing to do with whether the things described by the words have anything to do with men's lives or women's lives. Gender is simply a way of organising the words in the grammars of some languages. For example, in the ancient Roman language Latin, the word for table is *mensa* and it is a feminine noun. Clearly tables are not actually feminine and they are not only used by women. What is useful, in terms of Latin, about knowing that the word for table is feminine, is that then you also know that if you want to describe that table (for example, to say 'a white table'), you should use a particular type of descriptive word which matches the noun.

Secondly, the word 'gender' is used in the context of biology and scientific practice, where we talk about the gender of animals. In science, we use the word 'gender' to refer to whether the animal has male or female reproductive characteristics. In other words, we classify the animal according to its sex. We decide what sex it is based on the animal's anatomy. For example, and at its simplest, if a mammal has a penis we regard it as male. This is part of what the second dictionary definition means by 'the condition of being male or female.' Despite the dictionary's definition, many writers and theorists prefer to use the term 'sex' instead of 'gender' to refer to anatomical classification. This avoids confusing anatomy with other senses of 'gender'.

But in this chapter we will focus on another way of using the word 'gender'. This use of the word is hinted at by the dictionary definition's phrase 'the condition of being male or female', but it refers to far more than biological facts. This use of the word is similar to the scientific use we described, since it also relates to the idea of classification (describing according to different types). What is different about this use of the word, though, is that it refers to the way we describe human beings based on ideas about being female and ideas about being male, rather than based on the differences between men's and women's bodies.

In other words, gender refers to the concepts of femininity and masculinity which have been shaped by our societies, traditions, religions, families and education. Whereas biological sex refers to how we are constructed physically, gender refers to our social construction as men and women.

We all have ideas about the world we live in and the people we live with. These ideas affect the way we see ourselves and others. Usually we hold these ideas without consciously thinking about them – they become assumptions which affect our thinking. As a result, these assumptions affect our writing, reading and inter-preting of texts.

Often, we don't question our own assumptions unless we are faced with a personal crisis. For example, we might suddenly find that we have to face the fact that someone we love has become HIV-positive. We would have to look at what this means to us. In other words, we might have lived with the idea that 'it won't happen to me' but then find that our idea might be wrong. Our assumptions and confidence are shaken, and we have to look at our own lives carefully and seriously. What has happened here is a questioning of assumptions.

In this chapter we will focus on assumptions about gender, looking at what we take for granted when we write and read. We will also explore how assumptions about gender are part of the things we read.

Is sex gender?

Let's return to the idea mentioned earlier, that gender refers to the ideas we have about femaleness (femininity) and maleness (masculinity). Another way of expressing this would be to say that gender refers to processes of seeing and representing people based on sexual difference.

SEXUAL DIFFERENCE

The idea of sexual difference underlies the way we classify people as male or female. But 'male' and 'female' are biological categories. They refer to people's physical differences and to their different reproductive functions. In other words, male bodies and female bodies play different roles in conceiving and producing children. The 'sex' of a person is, then, a biological category. A person is described as being of the female or male sex on the basis of the kind of body (specifically what kind of sexual organs) she or he is born with.

For example, when my child was born, the doctor helping me announced excitedly 'you have a son'. The medical staff had to record the details of the birth and identify the baby, and wrote on the forms the description 'live male'. At that point, our baby's sex had been identified as male; he had been categorized or classed as male. I had spent many exhausting months waiting for the baby's birth without knowing whether a boy or a girl would be born, but now I had been given a label to apply to my child. 'The baby' was now 'my baby son'. I immediately found myself thinking about him in a way which was quite different from the ways I had thought during my pregnancy. I lay there recovering from the birth and trying to imagine what a little boy was, in a sense. I knew he was a 'live male', but part of me did not really know what that meant – it was just a label, just a description.

FROM SEX TO GENDER

A baby's sex might be identified as male, but the ways people then think about the baby will reflect their ideas about maleness. For instance, some people would feel unhappy about dressing a little newborn baby boy in pink clothing, because they believe that 'boys should wear blue, girls should wear pink'. This is an assumption about gender because it reflects ideas about what is right for maleness and what is right for femaleness.

Our assumptions about maleness and femaleness lead us to see and think about people in certain ways. Frequently people hold assumptions about women which lead them to think that women are naturally interested in domesticity, mothering and nurturing. They think that women are by nature more caring or sensitive than men and that they are weak and automatically inclined to choose roles in which they are powerless or passive. Similarly, they think that men are naturally strong, less caring, not interested in nurturing and more interested in physical activity. But these assumptions create stereotypes (or what we could call stereotyped views of masculinity and femininity). Assumptions of this sort affect our reactions to ideas or situations. However, our interpretations and perceptions are frequently based on prejudice, illogical thinking and unsound assumptions.

SEXUALITY

We do not usually think of someone as having a female or male 'sexuality'. 'Sexuality' usually refers to sexual orientation, or the choices that people make about having sex. When we describe someone as 'heterosexual', 'homosexual' or 'bisexual', we are referring to their sexuality rather than their sex. We also use 'sexuality' when we refer to sexual desire and sexual experience.

EVEN THE VERY ORDINARY interpretation of a person's sexuality on the basis of genital difference can be invalid and unsound. People are sometimes born with genitals that are formed in a way that is not clearly male or clearly female. For many years, medical practice dealt with this confusing situation by deciding that a child born with uncertain sexual characteristics should be classed as male, at least until the child's body developed other signs of a definite sex.

Beliefs about sexuality also reflect prejudices and assumptions. For instance, some people think that women are less interested in having sex than men. This is seen in the old story that during the Edwardian era in Britain, young women were advised by their mothers before getting married to 'shut their eyes and think of England' when having sex. Then there is the commonly held idea that men need to have many sexual partners while women only need or want one partner. But these beliefs can be seen as the result of the ways society has been organized for many years. Over time, certain ways of organizing people start to seem natural and inevitable. However, throughout history men have occupied more positions of power than women, and it is possible to see these ideas about sex as linked with this unequal distribution of power. Beliefs that allow men greater freedom of behaviour and impose restrictions on women support social and political arrangements that make men more powerful than women.

A strong influence on beliefs about sex and gender differences has been the tendency in some cultures to see women as valuable in terms of property. Women's ability to bear children has meant that they have been important in the processes of property inheritance. For instance, it was often thought necessary to control women's sexual activity in order to be sure that the children they produced were the children of the men who owned the property which the children would inherit one day. Chastity (that is, virginity and marital fidelity) became an important consideration. In this manner, ideas about what was 'natural' for women underpinned economic and power structures.

BORN TO HUNT

Many common assumptions are reflected in the following short extract. These assumptions are not expressed directly, since the writer uses metaphorical language to make her point. The writer speaks about relationships between men and women, but uses the metaphor of hunting to convey her ideas. After reading the extract, copy and complete the table. This table lists some of the assumptions that appear in the extract. Next to each assumption

MADE FOR EACH OTHER

write down what you feel about it or how you react to the ideas in the assumption.

 AN IS A HUNTER by nature. He likes to chase his game. His pleasure lies in the pursuit. With capture and possession there often comes lack of interest; so that the wise woman restrains herself at such passionate moments, in order that he may be kept eager in his pursuit.

FROM: Estelle Cole, *Education for Marriage*. 1938.
Quoted in Gerda Sian, *Gender, Sex and Sexuality*, p. 13.

Assumption	My feelings and reactions
A man is a hunter.	
A man likes to 'hunt' and to chase a woman.	
Although a man likes to chase a woman, he doesn't like actually succeeding.	
After he has successfully achieved a relationship with a woman, a man loses interest in her.	
A woman should play hard to get, because this will keep the man interested in her.	

THE WORD 'metaphorical' refers to our habit of using words in ways that are different from their obvious or 'literal' meanings. 'Metaphor' is language used to suggest that something is 'as if' it is something else, although the words 'as if' do not appear on the page. When a metaphor describes something – an idea or a person – as if it were something else, it suggests that there are similarities between it and the thing it is described as. It implies that they have the same characteristics and makes connections between things that are not necessarily or directly connected. Metaphors make descriptions in writing interesting and forceful, but this is not their only function. They convey ideas and allow for many possibilities of meaning.

TIME OFF
TO THINK!

❂ So, if faced with the question 'is sex gender?' what do you say? Summarize for yourself the difference between the terms 'sex' and 'gender'.
❂ Can you think of assumptions which you hold about maleness and femaleness? Make a list of your own assumptions.
❂ Do you see yourself as affected in your own life by assumptions that other people have about maleness and femaleness (gender)? Think about this question and use your ideas to help you complete this table (one example in each column has been filled in already).

What do some people assume about men?	What do some people assume about women?	Do I think this assumption is valid? Why?	Did or does this assumption affect my life?
Men are better leaders than women.		No, leadership qualities depend on a person's abilities, not on gender.	At work, men seem to get more promotions than women do.
	Women are more emotional than men.		

3 Hysteria and ideas about women

The word 'hysteria' is derived from the ancient Greek word for womb (*hystera*), which indicates that for centuries people have linked irrational behaviour with femaleness. Ancient Greek doctors, following the ideas of the famous doctor Hippocrates, thought that a woman's uterus did not always occur in a fixed spot in her body. They thought that it moved around in her body, and that this movement caused her body to react in various ways. In particular, when the womb reached the area around the heart, it blocked the blood flow and caused the woman to feel faint, excitable, short of breath and irrational. They said then that a woman was being *hysterikos*, or 'hysterical'. Relying on this idea about the uterus, the logic behind the invention of the term 'hysterical' would be: since it seems 'natural' for a woman to have a womb (uterus), it also seems 'natural' for her to behave hysterically. Because men do not normally have female sexual organs it also seemed unusual and almost impossible for a man to behave hysterically. It seemed 'unnatural' for a man to be hysterical. Behaviour of that sort, when performed by a man, would be called 'unmanly' and 'womanish'.

Influenced by the Greek idea, the ancient Romans referred to the woman's womb as an animal that needed to be driven back into its lair. This suggests that they saw the womb and its alleged effects as something dangerous and wild. It also suggests a view of women as threatening, inferior and animal-like, needing to be tamed. Roman medical practices included methods for treating illnesses related to the womb; they would apply substances and objects to the woman's body that were meant to push the womb back to where it was allegedly meant to be. These practices were brutal and caused great suffering for women. They also indicate that the ideas that people have about one another have deeply important consequences (results). In this example, such consequences could include physical pain and even death.

Beliefs about hysteria continued to focus on women for many years. People still thought of hysterical behaviour as typical of women. In the nineteenth century, the French doctor Jean Charcot conducted research into hysteria. The patients he studied were mostly women. The word 'hysteria' was used to describe illnesses such as blindness and speech loss when it was unclear what had caused the condition. Mysterious illnesses in this way became associated with the word 'hysteria', and with the idea of women.

Beliefs such as those about hysteria are 'made up', or, as we say academically, they are 'constructed' or 'produced'. In other words, they are not 'natural' in the same way that being born with female physical characteristics can be seen as natural. In academic discourse°, we talk about the construction or constructedness of beliefs to make the point that many of the ideas people have are the results of particular ways of thinking.

We tend to assume that many of our beliefs are natural and inescapable because 'the world is like that'. But many of our beliefs only appear to be natural and inevitable. Often what we believe is affected by the family-based, religious, economic, social and political networks that are part of our lives. It is useful to think about these factors that affect our thinking as structures. That is, we operate within many different kinds of relationships, which are all affected by various ideas. These ideas surround and support us in the same way that the structure of a house surrounds us; to some extent, a house's structure determines how we live and what we see. The ways in which we treat other people and they treat us are affected by such structures or ideas.

Jane Austen 1775-1817

Jane Austen wrote
but she never
To this very day she

Just in case you need persuasion, we're open 364 days a year, offer cakes, coffee and 25% off all hardcover fiction. You'll find

MADE FOR EACH OTHER

Text and gender

To start looking at text and gender, think about the advertisement shown at the bottom of pages 120–121. This is an advertisement for a chain of book shops. It uses wordplay to draw people's attention to the shops and their merchandise. But why is it written in this way?

✪ What is the point of informing us that the writer Jane Austen wrote about romances but did not get married?

✪ In what ways is she 'on the shelf'? Have you come across the phrase 'she is on the shelf' in other contexts, and do you know what it usually means?

✪ What view of Jane Austen do you think this advertisement encourages the reader to take?

✪ Do you think the advertisement supports or attacks stereotypes? Why?

Examining and challenging stereotypes is one of the focuses of feminism and the women's movement. Where unfair treatment and discrimination occur among people as the result of assumptions about gender, feminists protest against the beliefs and con-

The Jupiter Drawing Room 5950

novels about country romances married.
remains on the shelf.

us at The Firs of Rosebank, Balfour Park, Sandton Square, The Mall of Rosebank & Menlyn Park.

ditions that allow for this. They also object to the social systems in which women usually occupy positions that are inferior to men.

> **feminism** /'femənızəm/ n [U] (**a**) belief in the principle that women should have the same rights and opportunities as men. (**b**) the movement(5) in support of this.
> ► **feminist** /'femənıst/ n a supporter of feminism: *Suffragettes were among the first feminists in Britain and the USA.* ○ *He has strong feminist opinions.*
>
> **the 'women's movement** n [sing] the social and political movement promoting the idea that men and women should have equal rights in society, and aiming to achieve this by legal means and by changing people's attitudes.

Complete the following table as a way of examining your own ideas about feminism. In the first column, write down what you think are the characteristics of feminists (for example, you might think that feminists are women, and so would fill in 'women' in the first line). Try to think of as many descriptions as possible. In the second column, write down what you think feminists believe. Again, try to think of as many different ideas as possible.

Feminists are ...	Feminists believe ...

✪ Using what you have included in your table, write down your own definition of feminism.

✪ Think about the book shop's advertisement again. Do you see it positively or negatively, when you relate it to your concept of feminism?

The writer referred to in the advertisement, Jane Austen (1775-1817), lived and wrote in England. She published several novels which became famous and widely read. She has been seen as an important writer in the context of English literature. Significantly, her books were not originally published under her name; instead, the phrase 'By a Lady' appeared where the name of the author would normally be printed in the book. In spite of this, her identity as the author became known. When she died, her fame ensured that her family would be allowed the honour of burying her in Winchester Cathedral. But although this was a recognition of her significance as a writer, Jane Austen's family had the following written on her grave:

IN MEMORY OF
JANE AUSTEN
YOUNGEST DAUGHTER OF THE LATE
Revd. GEORGE AUSTEN
FORMERLY RECTOR OF STEVENTON IN THIS COUNTY.
SHE DEPARTED THIS LIFE ON THE 18TH. OF JULY 1817
AGED 41, AFTER A LONG ILLNESS SUPPORTED WITH
THE PATIENCE AND THE HOPES OF A CHRISTIAN.

THE BENEVOLENCE OF HER HEART
THE SWEETNESS OF HER TEMPERAMENT
THE EXTRAORDINARY ENDOWMENT OF HER MIND
OBTAINED THE REGARD OF ALL WHO KNEW HER AND
THE WARMEST LOVE OF HER INTIMATE CONNECTIONS.

THEIR GRIEF IS IN PROPORTION TO THEIR AFFECTION
THEY KNOW THEIR LOSS TO BE IRREPARABLE
BUT IN THEIR DEEPEST AFFLICTION THEY ARE CONSOLED
BY A FIRM THOUGH HUMBLE HOPE THAT HER CHARITY
DEVOTION, FAITH AND PURITY HAVE RENDERED
HER SOUL ACCEPTABLE IN THE SIGHT OF HER

REDEEMER

FROM: Margaret Kirkham, *Jane Austen: Feminism and Fiction*, p. 55. 1983. Sussex: Harvester.

The ideas that are emphasized in this description of the writer are worth thinking about.

✪ What image of her is presented by the description on her grave?
✪ Why do you think Jane Austen's father's position is so prominent on the gravestone? What do you think of this?

Think about the phrase 'By a Lady' used in place of Austen's name in her first books.

✪ What do you think about describing someone as a 'lady'?
✪ Who would you describe as a 'lady'?
✪ What qualities does this person have?
✪ Does 'lady' have a different meaning from 'woman'?

TIME OFF
TO THINK!

✪ Does gender influence all our thinking about people and about texts?
✪ When we read, is gender an issue only when the text represents men and women in ways that are clearly biased or prejudiced?

. . . .

TWO

CONSTRUCTING WORDS, CONSTRUCTING ROLES

IN THIS SECTION, we will focus on the idea that people play different roles, which are affected by ideas about gender. We will also look at some of the ways in which gender affects language and our speech patterns. The ideas and exercises in this section will help you to think about the effect of gender on people's roles. You will also explore the idea that words are affected by gender assumptions, and that gender influences the way we speak.

 Roles we play

What follows is a story which has no writer! At least, it does, but the writer has not decided exactly what shape the story will take.

Several paragraphs have been written, but it is up to you (the reader) to put them together. You will see how to do this by following the instructions, which appear like this:

✪ Do you scream in fear and try to hide behind your companion? (If yes, GO TO PARAGRAPH 2.)

All the paragraphs are separate and numbered, but they have not been printed in numerical order. In other words, we have deliberately mixed up the order in which they appear. You will have to check the beginning of each paragraph carefully to see which number it is. Every paragraph has instructions in it about which one to move on to – except for paragraphs 14, 15 and 16, which are all possible conclusions for the story. All you need to do is follow these instructions and look for the paragraph you want.

What you need to decide before you start to read and connect the paragraphs is whether you want to pretend to be the character called Harry (who is a man) or the character called Sally (who is a woman). Try to imagine that you are the character you choose to be. You will need to make your choices, when you face choices in the story, by thinking what you would do if you were Harry or if you were Sally. Once you have gone through the story as one character, try reading it again as the other character, and see whether your choices remain the same.

It is a dark and stormy night ...

1 IT IS A DARK AND STORMY NIGHT, a typical Highveld summer evening. All the long, hot afternoon the clouds have piled up and crashed into each other, and now their blackened mass looms over the landscape. A small yellow car can

be seen travelling along an otherwise empty road. The car's two occupants are a man and a woman. Harry and Sally (for those are their names) look at each other. Each is thinking about the coming storm. They smile, but clearly both are a little nervous about the weather. Now, as the lightning cuts through the dark sky, the car sputters, jerks and stops. There they are, alone on a tarred road, darkness around, the veld stretching into the lonely distance. 'What do we do now?' one of them says.

'Oh, I can fix it – just move out of my way.'

'It's so lucky you are here! I am no good at this sort of thing ...'

Anyway, despite these brave efforts, the car is not fixed after an hour. Its occupants, Harry and Sally, decide that the problem is probably that the car has run out of petrol. They are both wet and unhappy and decide they must go in search of help – and petrol. Suddenly a flash of lightning lights up the sky and they see a large house looming darkly against the horizon. It is not far away, and they decide to walk to it and ask for help. On reaching the house, they knock on the door. After a few minutes it opens. The room they see is huge and dark, lit only by a few candles. A tall man with bright purple hair stands facing them. In his hands is a gun – it is not pointed at them but Harry and Sally both notice it gleaming in the candlelight. The purple-haired man smiles strangely and shouts, 'Surprise!'

✪ Do you scream in fear and try to hide behind your companion? (If yes, GO TO PARAGRAPH 2.)

✪ Do you move into the house confidently and say, 'Hello, our car has broken down. Please help us'? (If yes, GO TO PARAGRAPH 3.)

✪ Do you tell your companion to step aside, then grab the gun and point it at the purple-haired man? (If yes, GO TO PARAGRAPH 4.)

6 The person's hand is quickly withdrawn. You smile nervously and turn around, looking for your partner.

✪ GO TO PARAGRAPH 9.

2   When you scream, the purple-haired man laughs and reaches his hand out to you. 'Come inside, my dears. Don't worry about the gun, it's just a silly toy!' he says. You both enter the room. It is strange and gloomy, but as your eyes adjust to the shadows, you notice that it is full of people, all dressed unusually but smiling, drinking, eating and chatting softly to one another. Slowly, you realize that you have not stumbled into a house full of dangerous people with evil intent – no, this is a party!

✪ GO TO PARAGRAPH 5.

3   You find yourself in a strange and gloomy room, but as your eyes adjust to the shadows, you notice that it is full of people, all dressed unusually but smiling, drinking, eating and chatting softly to one another. Slowly, you realize that you have not stumbled into a house full of dangerous people with evil intent – no, this is a party! You realize you can stop worrying about why the purple-haired man was carrying a gun: he wasn't afraid of being attacked, as it was clearly not a real gun, simply a silly toy. After all, people do odd things at parties, you think to yourself.

✪ GO TO PARAGRAPH 5.

8   The person's hand is quickly withdrawn. You smile triumphantly and turn around, looking for your partner.

✪ GO TO PARAGRAPH 9.

5   Someone comes up to you, embraces you, puts a glass of something delicious in your hand, and offers you food. A feeling of happiness settles on you as slowly you forget your unpleasant experiences. You find yourself thinking that it would be nice to spend a little time here, and you forget about getting petrol for the car. Your clothes dry out, you sit down, relax and talk to the people around you, who are actually quite friendly and interesting. But suddenly you realize that there is a hand on

your leg and it is not yours. You look up and see a face grinning at you; it is the kind of face people dream of, everything a lover should look like.

- ✪ Do you smile at the person regretfully and say, 'Sorry, I am with someone else'? (If yes, GO TO PARAGRAPH 6.)
- ✪ Do you smile seductively and ask the person to fetch you something to drink? (If yes, GO TO PARAGRAPH 7.)
- ✪ Do you glare at the person and say, 'Touch me again and you'll be sorry'? (If yes, GO TO PARAGRAPH 8.)

4 The gun is in your hands, you are pointing it at the purple-haired man. He looks less frightened than you expect, in fact he still smiles oddly. You begin to worry, your heart beats faster as you think there must be someone behind you, someone who also has a gun. Quickly, you turn around and attempt to overpower the person you think is behind you. But ... you fall face down on the ground, the gun flies out of your hand, and you hear, again, that strange laugh. This time, though, the man bends down and helps you to your feet. 'Come inside, my dears,' he says. You both enter the room. It is strange and gloomy, but as your eyes adjust to the shadows, you notice that it is full of people, all dressed unusually but smiling, drinking, eating and chatting to one another. Slowly, you realize that you have not stumbled into a house full of dangerous people with evil intent – no, this is a party!

- ✪ GO TO PARAGRAPH 5.

14 You think about things for a while and decide that it has been an interesting night. The petrol container is in your hand, you suddenly realize, so you leave the house and start to make your way back to your abandoned car. Around you, the veld is being lit by the cold, grey light of dawn. The sun is rising, leaving behind a night that has been long, dark and stormy.

10 You spend time in the pool, but then notice your companion standing next to the pool looking at you with unusual intensity. You feel embarrassed. You decide it is time to get out, which you do. Unfortunately, your companion has disappeared by now. After finding your clothes and getting dressed, you go into the room and settle down in a large, comfortable chair.

✪ GO TO PARAGRAPH 13.

7 Is this a new relationship starting for you? This person is fun, interesting, attractive. You dance together, laugh, talk and enjoy yourselves. You forget about the person who was with you in the car when you arrived.

✪ GO TO PARAGRAPH 9.

12 You go back into the room, where you think about the other people swimming and wonder when your companion will come and find you. You settle down in a large, comfortable chair.

✪ GO TO PARAGRAPH 13.

15 You think about things for a while and decide that it has been a tiring night. Your companion smiles at you and says, 'Well, that was interesting!' You notice that the petrol container is in your hand, so you leave the house and start to make your way back to your abandoned car. Around you, the veld is being lit by the cold, grey light of dawn. The sun is rising, leaving behind a night that has been long, dark and stormy.

9 A loud noise outside the room catches your attention. Shouting and laughing fill the air. You move to the window and see a swimming pool; many of the partygoers are jumping into it. The storm has finished and the evening is lovely – perfect weather for a late night swim. You notice your companion going out to the pool and you decide to follow.

Suddenly the purple-haired man appears again. This time he is naked. He grabs your arm, says, 'Come on, let's swim!' and suggests you take off your clothes too.

✪ Do you throw off all your clothes and jump delightedly into the pool? (If yes, GO TO PARAGRAPH 10.)
✪ Do you keep all your clothes on but jump delightedly into the pool? (If yes, GO TO PARAGRAPH 11.)
✪ Do you smile, say, 'No thanks,' and leave the pool area? (If yes, GO TO PARAGRAPH 12.)

11 You spend time in the pool, until you decide you are tired of the feeling of swimming in wet, heavy clothes. You notice your companion standing next to the pool looking at you with unusual intensity. You decide it is time to get out, which you do. Unfortunately, your companion has disappeared by now. You go into the room and settle down in a large, comfortable chair, hoping your clothes will soon dry out.

✪ GO TO PARAGRAPH 13.

13 Time passes. You notice that the other people in the room are all sitting in groups of two or three, chatting companionably. You begin to feel lonely and wonder where your companion is. Then you remember why you came to this house in the first place and ask the purple-haired man (who has suddenly appeared again) if he can help you get some petrol. 'No problem,' he says. After half an hour he returns with a large plastic container of petrol, which he gives to you. Then you see your companion enter the room, holding hands with someone else. They walk over to your chair, and your companion immediately starts talking to you.

✪ Do you get up and leave without listening? (If yes, GO TO PARAGRAPH 14.)
✪ Do you get up, grab your companion's arm and leave the room? (If yes, GO TO PARAGRAPH 15.)
✪ Do you say to them, 'Let's go and talk outside,' and walk out of the room? (If yes, GO TO PARAGRAPH 16.)

16 You think about things for a while and decide that it has been an exhausting night. You notice that the petrol container is in your hand, so you leave the house and start to make your way back to your abandoned car. Are you alone or not? By this stage, you hardly care enough to notice. Home is where you want to be. Around you, the veld is being lit by the cold, grey light of dawn. The sun is rising, leaving behind a night that has been long, dark and stormy.

When you read the story called 'It is a dark and stormy night ...'
✪ Do you think your choices were affected by the role you chose to play?
✪ Were the decisions you made as you went through the story influenced by ideas about how you think a man or woman would behave in those situations?
✪ Has your experience of this story affected your ideas about gender in any way?

② Speaking of gender

According to some people, how we speak to one another and describe ourselves often reveals the effect that gender has on our lives (even when we are unconscious of these effects). This is controversial, since not everyone would agree with theories which claim that gender affects the way we speak. But we shall be looking at an article in which the writer does claim that gender affects the ways in which women speak. The writer presents a strong argument and takes a polemical° standpoint.

Before reading it, though, it would be useful to think briefly about your own ways of speaking. Do you think they might be affected by your gender? For example, do you think you have any noticeable habits when you ask people questions? If you have ideas about these issues at this point, write them down and look back at them after you have read the article 'You Are What You Say'.

You Are What You Say

by Robin Lakoff

'WOMEN'S LANGUAGE' is that pleasant, never-aggressive way of talking we learned as little girls. Cultural bias was built into the language we were allowed to speak, the subjects we were allowed to speak about, and the ways we were spoken of. Having learned our linguistic lesson well, we go out into the world only to discover that we are communicative cripples – damned if we do, and damned if we don't.

If we refuse to talk 'like a lady' we are ridiculed and criticized for being unfeminine. ('She thinks like a man' is, at best, a back-handed compliment.) If we do learn all the unassertive language of our sex, we are ridiculed for being unable to think clearly, unable to take part in a serious discussion, and therefore unfit to hold a position of power.

It doesn't take much of this for a woman to begin feeling she deserves such treatment because of inadequacies in her own intelligence and education.

Women's language

'Women's language' shows up in all levels of English. For example, women are encouraged and allowed to describe far more precise differences in naming colours than men do. Words like mauve, beige, aquamarine, lavender, and so on, are more often used by women than by men. I know of no scientific evidence that women actually see a wider range of colours than men do. It is simply that fine differences of this sort are relevant to women's vocabularies but not to men's. To men, who control most of the interesting affairs of the world, such distinctions are trivial and irrelevant.

In the area of syntax we find similar gender-related peculiarities of speech. There is one construction in particular that women use conversationally far more than men: the tag-question. A statement indicates that the speaker is confident about his/her knowledge and is fairly certain to be believed. A question indicates a lack of knowledge on some point and implies that there is a gap in the speaker's knowledge which can be fixed by an answer. A tag question is a statement that doesn't have to be believed by anyone but the speaker. It is a way of not forcing the listener to go along with the views of the speaker. In a tag question, the speaker is wanting the listener to agree with the opinions rather than the facts. An example would be, 'The situation in Southeast Asia is terrible, isn't it?'

There are other ways to interpret a sentence like this, but one possible interpretation is that the speaker has a particular answer in mind – 'yes' or 'no' – but is reluctant to state it baldly. In conversations, this sort of tag question is much more likely to be used by women than by men. Why is this the case?

The tag question allows the speaker to avoid commitment, and so to avoid conflict with the listener. The problem is that, by doing this, the speaker may give the impression of lacking confidence, or wanting support from the listener for his/her opinions. The person being addressed is put in the position of having to provide confirmation.

One likely result of a woman using this sort of speech pattern is that, often without knowing it, the speaker builds a reputation of tentativeness. Other people will not take her seriously or trust her with any real responsibilities since they think she 'can't make up her mind,' and 'isn't sure of herself.'

Polite women

Such habits may explain why women's language often sounds much more 'polite' than men's language. It is polite to leave a decision open, and not force your ideas, or views, or claims on anyone else. So a tag question is a kind of polite statement, in that it does not force agreement or belief on the listener.

In the same way, a request is a polite command, because it does not force obedience on the listener. Rather, it suggests that something be done as a favour to the speaker. The speaker implies that if the request is not carried out, only the speaker will suffer. So the decision is really left up to the listener. The differences become clear in these examples (compare the first two statements with the last three tag questions):

Close the door.	Will you close the door?
Please close the door.	Will you please close the door?
	Won't you close the door?

Describing women

The words and speech patterns used by a woman often undermine her image, but those used to describe women make matters even worse. Often a word may be used to refer to both men and women (and perhaps things as well). However, when it is applied to women, it takes on a special meaning that, by implication rather than direct assertion, is derogatory to women as a group.

The use of euphemisms has this effect. A euphemism is a substitute for a word that has acquired a bad connotation by association with something unpleasant or embarrassing. But almost as soon as the new word comes into common usage, it takes on the same old bad connotations since feelings about the things or people referred to are not altered by a change of name.

Ladies and gentlemen

There is one euphemism for 'woman' still very much alive. The word of course, is 'lady'. 'Lady' has a masculine counterpart, namely 'gentleman', occasionally shortened to 'gent'.

But for some reason 'lady' is far more common than 'gent' or 'gentleman'.

To say 'lady doctor' is very condescending, since no one ever says 'gentleman doctor' or even 'man doctor'. For example, a mention in the San Francisco Chronicle of 31 January 1972, of Madalyn Murray O'Hair as 'the lady atheist' makes her seem silly and unusual. Even 'woman atheist' is not an acceptable description: sex is irrelevant to her philosophical position.

Many women argue that, on the other hand, 'lady' carries with it the idea of the age of chivalry; they say that it gives the person referred to a special status. This makes the term seem polite at first, but we must also remember that these implications are problematic: they suggest that a 'lady' is helpless and cannot do things by herself.

'Lady' can also be used to suggest a lack of seriousness, as in titles of organizations. Organizations that have a serious purpose (not simply giving 'the ladies' a chance to spend time together) cannot use the word 'lady' in their titles, but less serious ones may. Compare the 'Ladies' Auxiliary' of a men's group, or the 'Thursday Evening Ladies' Browning and Garden Society', with 'Ladies' Liberation' or 'Ladies' Strike for Peace'.

The comfort of euphemisms

What is curious about this split is that 'lady' is in origin a euphemism. It is a substitute that puts a better face on something people sometimes find uncomfortable – the word 'woman'. Perhaps 'lady' functions as a euphemism for 'woman' because it does not contain the sexual implications present in 'woman': it is not 'embarrassing' in that way.

Another common substitute for 'woman' is 'girl'. A man who is past the age of adolescence is not usually called a boy, except in expressions like 'going out with the boys'. Such an expression is meant to suggest an air of adolescent fun and irresponsibility. But women of all ages are called 'girls'. It may be that this use of 'girl' is euphemistic in the same way the use of 'lady' is. In stressing the idea of immaturity it removes the sexual connotations lurking in 'woman'.

'Girl' brings to mind irresponsibility: you don't send a girl to do a woman's task (or even a boy's task). She is a person who is too immature to be entrusted with responsibilities or with important decisions.

Finally, why is it that shop assistants and others are so quick to call women customers 'dear', 'honey', and other terms of endearment they really have no right to use? A male customer would never put up with it. But women, like children, are supposed to enjoy these endearments, rather than being offended by them.

In more ways than one, it's time to speak up.

ADAPTED FROM the version appearing in James D. Lester (Ed.), *Daughters of the Revolution*. 1996. NTC Publishing Group. Reprinted there from *Ms.* magazine, 1974, by permission of Robin Lakoff.

This article raises some important and controversial issues. Copy and complete the following paragraphs, which focus on the points made by the writer:

- ✪ Lakoff introduces the idea of 'women's language'. She uses this phrase to describe the ways in which …
- ✪ She claims that there is a difference between statements and questions. This difference is …
- ✪ However, she also discusses tag questions. Tag questions are … Tag questions affect women by …
- ✪ Lakoff argues that the way women speak often sounds more polite than the way men speak. This is because …
- ✪ Euphemisms are used when …
- ✪ However, Lakoff thinks that a euphemism such as the word 'lady' is problematic because …
- ✪ Lakoff concludes by claiming that …

MADE FOR EACH OTHER

Try to decide how you feel about the ideas expressed in the article – in other words, do you think that the writer is correct? If you think that the writer's ideas are wrong, try to think of ways to show her that she is wrong. To do this, you would need to think of examples and ideas which would support your opinion. In order to focus your mind on what you think about the article, answer these questions:

❂ How do you react to the ideas presented in this article?

❂ Do you agree or disagree with the basic claim that people use language differently because of their gender differences?

❂ Have you heard or thought about these ideas in the past, and do you find them interesting?

❂ What do you think about the writer's claim that 'Even "woman atheist" is not an acceptable description: sex is irrelevant to her philosophical position'? Why is sex 'irrelevant'? Do you agree with this statement?

 Resisting prejudice

Now that we have had a look at how assumptions about gender may be reflected in the English language, we will focus on the ways women have expressed in writing their frustration about society's unfair treatment of women and the double standards° that apply to women.

The poem printed on the following page refers openly to factors and problems that affect the lives of millions of women (and therefore the lives of the men and children with whom women share their lives). Read through the poem. If there are words or phrases you do not understand, you might find it useful to underline them. If you use a dictionary to look up the meanings, remember to select a meaning that fits the context. When you have done this, read through the poem again. You might like to read it aloud to yourself or to someone else. Often, it is easier to understand a text when you hear the words read aloud.

BECAUSE WE'RE WOMEN
Sonya Meyer

Because women's work is never done
and is underpaid and boring
or repetitious and we're the first to
get the sack and what we
look like is more important than what
we do and if we get raped
it's our fault and if we get bashed we
must have provoked it and
if we raise our voices we're nagging
bitches and if we enjoy sex
we're nymphos and if we don't we're
frigid and if we love women
it's because we can't get a 'real' man
and if we ask our doctor
too many questions we're neurotic
and/or pushy and if we expect
community care for our children we're
selfish and if we stand up
for our rights we're aggressive and
'unfeminine' and if we want to
get married we're out to trap a man
and if we don't we're
unnatural because we still can't
get an adequate, safe contraceptive
but men can walk on the
moon and if we can't cope or don't
want a pregnancy we're made to feel
guilty about abortion and ...
for lots of other reasons we
are part of the women's liberation
movement.

FROM: *Herstoria*, Summer
1996, Vol. 2 No. 3.

Do we usually expect that texts such as poems, plays and novels are politically neutral? Do politics have anything to do with the texts we read?

It is accurate, I think, to say that writers do engage with political issues. The poem 'Because we're women' seems to have a deliberate political intention, since it provokes the reader to respond to the issues to which it refers. This is a poem of protest and resistance in the context of gender issues, and it uses phrases which have often been used in the context of the women's movement. The poet uses descriptions and accusations which are usually used to criticize women. However, she undermines those ideas. She uses the very words with which women are abused, oppressed and judged to resist such abuse, oppression and judgement. In other words, she refers to the perspectives that devalue and discriminate against women in such a way that it is clear that she does not agree with these viewpoints. Her anger against such viewpoints leads to her final claim that these are the reasons for being 'part of the women's liberation / movement.'

PITY THE MEN OF TODAY:
Fay Weldon asks: Has feminism gone too far?

Perhaps feminism goes too far? Perhaps the pendulum has stuck and needs nudging back to a more moderate position? Our young men, it seems are in a sorry state: under-achieving in educational matters, if we are to believe a new British report, from the age of four. Parents don't bother to read to boys, apparently.

Let me put it like this. Young Nineties men complain that they are in a hopeless double bind. They care desperately for the good opinion of women. They want nothing more than to live a domestic life. If they show sensitivity, strive to be New Men, they are despised as wimps. If they keep a stiff upper lip, they are derided for their insensitivity.

Women, young men complain, want them for only one thing. They find themselves treated as sex objects. If they make sexual overtures, they are accused of harassment. If they don't, the same thing happens.

If he wants children, he has to search for a woman prepared to give him one. If he succeeds, if the woman doesn't have a termination with no reference to him, he is expected to bond with the baby and do his share of child-rearing, but is given no rights if the relationship goes wrong.

FROM: *Mail & Guardian*
23–29 January 1998

KEEPING TRACK
Denise Levertov

Between chores –
    hulling strawberries,
    answering letters –
or between poems,

returning to the mirror
to see if I'm there.

FROM: *Searching for Words*. 1970.
New York: New Directions.

How do you respond to Sonya Meyer's poem? Perhaps you agree with the ideas and feelings expressed in it, or with some of them but not all. On the other hand, you might object strongly to the poem's ideas or to the way it is written. Think back to the ideas about feminism raised in the first section of this chapter. In what ways does this poem relate to ideas you developed then about feminism? Is there anything you would now add to your definition, or any other way you would modify your definition?

NATURAL AND UNNATURAL

The poem 'Because we're women' refers to the accusation that a woman who does not want to marry is behaving in a way that is 'unnatural'. Think about your own notions of what is 'natural', or what 'human nature' is. You probably have many ideas about this, and certainly they will not all relate to gender or be easy to summarize. When we choose to call things natural or unnatural, our choices are often affected by other beliefs and assumptions which are part of our belief systems and world-views. Often we tend to think that what we label 'unnatural' is evil, bad or wicked. Similarly, we assume that what we think is 'natural' must be good. In the context of exploring gender ideas, we could ask ourselves the following questions. (Our answers would probably depend to a lesser or greater extent on some of our own, individual and deeply held beliefs.)

- ✪ Is it natural for a woman to want to get married?
- ✪ Is it natural for a man to want to get married?
- ✪ Do you think that we are genetically programmed at birth to behave in specific ways?
- ✪ What are the implications (or consequences) of regarding someone as unnatural or that person's choices as unnatural?

Write your own poem or paragraph(s) in which you express your own ideas on any of the issues raised in this section. What do you find interesting in the pieces you have read? Do you have opinions to express in response to any of the ideas they raise? You do not have to write in the same sort of style or express the same sort of opinions as these pieces. Try to write in your own 'voice' in a way that expresses your ideas.

TIME OFF
TO THINK!

Are we always inevitably influenced by gender? Does gender trap us when we want to speak or write?

. . . .

IN THIS SECTION we will focus on the idea that people want space in which to think, read and write. Sometimes this is physical space, but often it is not only physical space. People also want to find other abstract or figurative° kinds of space.

THREE

ROOM NEEDED

The ideas and exercises in this section will help you to relate the idea of space to gender, and to think about the kinds of space you do or do not have yourself.

① A room of one's own

One of the ideas that has shaped people's thinking about gender issues is the concept of 'a room of one's own'. The British novelist Virginia Woolf wrote a lecture in 1929 entitled *A Room of One's Own*. She looked at the way that women were traditionally not encouraged or enabled to write: fewer women than men were given education, and women's education was usually inferior to that of men and focused on skills such as housekeeping and hobbies. She claimed that people face material (physical) difficulties when wanting to write, such as poverty and not having a quiet, private place in which to sit and write. They lacked 'a room of their own'. But men, she said, were able to overcome these difficulties more easily than women, because women were often not as easily able to be economically independent.

Woolf went further though. She claimed that

EQUAL RIGHTS!

The Bill of Rights of the South African Constitution states:

(3) The state may not unfairly discriminate directly or indirectly against anyone on one or more grounds, including race, gender, sex, pregnancy, marital status, ethnic or social origin, colour, sexual orientation, age, disability, religion, conscience, belief, culture, language and birth.

(4) No person may unfairly discriminate directly or indirectly against anyone on one or more grounds in terms of sub-section (3) National legislation must be enacted to prevent or prohibit unfair discrimination.

(5) Discrimination on one or more of the grounds listed in subsection (3) is unfair unless it is established that the discrimination is fair.

Another provision of the Bill of Rights relates to freedom of expression. It is significant, though, that the concept of freedom of expression is also limited in various ways, and has some bearing on gender. For the Bill of Rights prohibits 'advocacy of hatred that is based on race, ethnicity, gender or religion, and that constitutes incitement to cause harm'.

such material difficulties were formidable; but much worse were the immaterial. The indifference of the world which ... men of genius have found so hard to bear was [for a woman writer] not indifference but hostility. The world did not say to her as it said to them, Write if you choose; it makes no difference to me. The world said with a [laugh], Write? What's the good of your writing?

ADAPTED FROM: Virginia Woolf, *A Room of One's Own*, p. 137. 1929. London: Harcourt Brace & Company.

Many other writers have explored the idea of 'a room of one's own' in the years since Woolf wrote. The idea has been used in different ways and for different purposes. For example, Carolyn Heilbrun, an American academic and writer of detective fiction, believes that

women have long searched, and continue to search, for an identity 'other' than their own. Caught in the conventions of their sex, they have sought an escape from gender.

She speaks about herself and her decision to write detective novels in a way that is similar to Virginia Woolf's idea of a room of one's own:

> I believe now that I must have wanted ... to create a space for myself .... I used to notice, visiting in the suburbs, that there was a room for everyone but the wife/mother, who, it was assumed, had the whole house .... If there was no space for a woman in the suburban dream house, how unlikely that there would be space in a small city apartment. So I wanted, I now guess, psychic space. ... [In writing novels] I was recreating myself.
>
> ADAPTED FROM: Carolyn G. Heilbrun, *Writing a Woman's Life*. 1988. W. W. Norton & Company.

The two writers I have referred to are talking specifically about the problems facing women who want to write. But, of course, gender issues are not simply about women. Gender affects our ideas of ourselves, and other people's ideas about us, whether we are men or women. Unfair discrimination on the grounds of sex and gender affects everyone.

Have you experienced the kinds of things that Virginia Woolf and Carolyn Heilbrun refer to in these extracts? Think about the following statements taken from them, and then complete the questions that follow:

✪ 'Material difficulties were formidable; but much worse were the immaterial.'

✪ 'Caught in the conventions of their sex, they have sought an escape from gender.'

✪ 'Write? What's the good of your writing?'

✪ 'I wanted ... to create a space for myself.'

✪ 'I was recreating myself.'

✪ Do you face physical difficulties in your own life when it comes to finding space to read, write and study?

✪ Do you also face other figurative, more abstract difficulties, such as having little time to spend on these activities or feeling that there are other obligations or pressures in your life that prevent you from studying, reading and writing?

✪ Copy and complete the following table to explore and list such difficulties. Think about the obstacles you face when you need to find 'a room for yourself'.

The difficulties I face in my physical space	The difficulties I face in my figurative space

✪ Can you see ways in which your two kinds of space affect each other?

✪ If you had 'a room of your own', what would you be able to do in such a space? Copy and complete the following table by listing the things that would enable you to have 'a room of your own' and what uses you would make of it.

How I would be able to have 'a room of my own'	What I would be able to do in 'a room of my own'

2 Room to write

Gcina Mhlophe is a South African writer and actor. In chapter two we looked at one of her poems, 'The Dancer'. Here we will discuss one of her short stories.

While at high school she wrote poems and stories in Xhosa, and when she lived in Johannesburg as a young woman she wrote and published stories in English. At this time, she did much of her reading and writing in a public toilet in Johannesburg. One of the stories she wrote is entitled 'The Toilet'. Read this short story and think about the issues discussed so far in this chapter. Also think how 'The Toilet' relates to the points on autobiographical writing raised in chapter one.

It's very important for women to write what they feel. Really, we need more writing from women. I think women understand each other better when they are alone together than when there's a man around because then there's always the possibility of pretending and that's not communication ... So we should come together as women and try to do some creative writing, I mean writing that will help or encourage other people who might become our fellow-writers in the future.

GCINA MHLOPHE, 'Men Are Always Women's Children'. Quoted in MJ Daymond 'Gender and "History": 1980s South African women's stories in English.' In *Ariel*, January 1996.

✪ What do you think about Gcina Mhlophe's ideas? Do you agree with her?

✪ Do you think we need 'more writing from women'?

✪ If we replaced 'women' with 'men' and 'man' with 'woman' where these words appear in her paragraph, would you agree or disagree with the ideas expressed?

✪ What other ideas do you have about this passage?

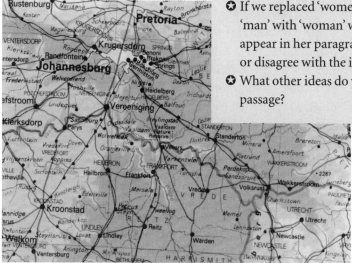

The Toilet

Gcina Mhlophe

SOMETIMES I wanted to give up and be a good girl who listened to her elders. Maybe I should have done something like teaching or nursing as my mother wished. People thought these professions were respectable, but I knew I wanted to do something different, though I was not sure what. I thought a lot about acting. ... My mother said that it had been a waste of good money educating me because I did not know what to do with the knowledge I had acquired. I'd come to Johannesburg for the December holidays after writing my matric exams, and then stayed on, hoping to find something to do.

My elder sister worked in Orange Grove as a domestic worker, and I stayed with her in her back room. I didn't know anybody in Jo'burg except my sister's friends whom we went to church with. The Methodist church up Fourteenth Avenue was about the only outing we had together. I was very bored and lonely.

On weekdays I was locked in my sister's room so that the Madam wouldn't see me. She was at home most of the time: painting her nails, having tea with her friends, or lying in the sun by the swimming pool. The swimming pool was very close to the room, which is why I had to keep very quiet. My sister felt bad about locking me in there, but she had no alternative. I couldn't even play the radio, so she brought me books, old magazines, and newspapers from the white people. I just read every single thing I came across: *Fair Lady*, *Woman's Weekly*, anything. But then my sister thought I was reading too much.

'What kind of wife will you make if you can't even make baby clothes, or knit yourself a jersey? I suppose you will marry an educated man like yourself, who won't mind going to bed with a book and an empty stomach.'

We would play cards at night when she knocked off, and listen to the radio, singing along softly with the songs we liked.

Then I got this temporary job in a clothing factory in town. I looked forward to meeting new people, and liked the idea of being out of that room for a change. The factory made clothes for ladies' boutiques.

The whole place was full of machines of all kinds. Some people were sewing, others were ironing with big heavy irons that pressed with a lot of steam. I had to cut all the loose threads that hang after a dress or a jacket is finished. As soon as a number of dresses in a certain style were finished, they would be sent to me and I had to count them, write the number down, and then start with the cutting of the threads. I was fascinated to discover that one person made only sleeves, another the collars, and so on until the last lady put all the pieces together, sewed on buttons, or whatever was necessary to finish.

Most people at the factory spoke Sotho, but they were nice to me – they tried to speak to me in Zulu or Xhosa, and they gave me all kinds of advice on things I didn't know. There was this girl, Gwendolene – she thought I was very stupid – she called me a 'bari' because I always sat inside the changing room with something to read when it was time to eat my lunch, instead of going outside to meet guys. She told me it was cheaper to get myself a 'lunch boy' – some-body to buy me lunch. She told me it was wise not to sleep with him, because then I could dump him anytime I wanted to. I was very nervous about such things. I thought it was better to be a 'bari' than to be stabbed by a city boy for his money.

The factory knocked off at four-thirty, and then I went to a park near where my sister worked. I waited there till half past six, when I could sneak into the house again without the white people seeing me. I had to leave the house before half past five in the mornings as well. That meant I had to find something to do with the time I had before I could catch the seven-thirty bus to work – about two hours. I would go to a public toilet in the park. For some reason it was never locked, so I would go in and sit on the toilet seat to read some magazine or other until the right time to catch the bus.

The first time I went into this toilet, I was on my way to the bus stop. Usually I went straight to the bus stop outside the OK Bazaars where it was well lit, and I could see. I would wait there, reading, or just looking at the growing number of cars and buses on their way to town. On this day it was raining quite hard, so I thought I would shelter in the toilet until the rain had passed. I knocked first to see if there was anyone inside. As there was no reply, I pushed the door open and went in. It smelled a little – a dryish kind of smell, as if the toilet was not used all that often, but it was quite clean compared to many 'Non-European' toilets I knew. The floor was painted red and the walls were cream white. It did not look like it had been painted for a few years. I stood looking around, with the rain coming very hard on the zinc roof. The noise was comforting – to know I had escaped the wet – only a few of the heavy drops had got me. The plastic bag in which I carried my book and purse and neatly folded pink handkerchief was a little damp, but that was because I had used it to cover my head when I ran to the toilet. I pulled my dress down a little so that it would not get creased when I sat down. The closed lid of the toilet was going to be my seat for many mornings after that.

I was really lucky to have found that toilet because the winter was very cold. Not that it was any warmer in there, but once I'd closed the door it used to be a little less windy. Also the toilet was very small – the walls were wonderfully close to me – it felt like it was made to fit me alone. I enjoyed that kind of privacy. I did a lot of thinking while I sat on that toilet seat. I did a lot of daydreaming too – many times imagining myself in some big hall doing a really popular play with other young actors. At school, we took set books like *Buzani KuBawo* or *A Man for All Seasons* and made school plays which we toured to the other schools on weekends. I loved it very much. When I was even younger I had done little sketches taken from the Bible and on big days like Good Friday, we acted and sang happily.

I would sit there dreaming. ...

I was getting bored with the books I was reading – the love stories all sounded the same, and besides that I just lost interest. I started asking myself why I had not written anything since I left school. At least at school I had written some poems, or stories for the school magazine, school competitions and other magazines like *Bona* and *Inkqubela*. Our English teacher was always so encouraging; I remembered the day I showed him my first poem – I was so excited I couldn't concentrate in class for the whole day. I didn't know anything about publishing then, and I didn't ask myself if my stories were good enough. I just enjoyed writing things down when I had the time. So one Friday, after I'd started being that toilet's best customer, I bought myself a notebook in which I was hoping to write something. I didn't use it for quite a while, until one evening.

My sister had taken her usual Thursday afternoon off, and she had been delayed somewhere. I came back from work, then waited in the park for the right time to go back into the yard. The white people always had their supper at six-thirty and that was the time I used to steal my way in without disturbing them or being seen. My comings and goings had to be secret because they still didn't know I stayed there.

Then I realized that she hadn't come back, and I was scared to go out again, in case something went wrong this time. I decided to sit down in front of my sister's room, where I thought I wouldn't be noticed. I was reading a copy of *Drum Magazine* and hoping that she would come back soon – before the dogs sniffed me out. For the first time I realized how stupid it was of me not to have cut myself a spare key long ago. I kept on hearing noises that sounded like the gate opening. A few times I was sure I had heard her footsteps on the concrete steps leading to the servant's quarters, but it turned out to be something or someone else.

I was trying hard to concentrate on my reading again, when I heard the two dogs playing, chasing each other nearer and nearer to where I was sitting. And then, there they were in front of me, looking as surprised as I was. For a brief moment we stared at each other, then they started to bark at me. I was sure they would tear me to pieces if I moved just one finger, so I sat very still, trying not to look at them, while my heart pounded and my mouth went dry as paper.

They barked even louder when the dogs from next door joined in, glared at me through the openings in the hedge. Then the Madam's high-pitched voice rang out above the dogs' barking.

'Ireeeeeeeene!' That's my sister's English name, which we never use. I couldn't move or answer the call – the dogs were standing right in front of me, their teeth so threateningly long. When there was no reply, she came to see what was going on.

'Oh, it's you? Hello.' She was smiling at me, chewing that gum which never left her mouth, instead of calling the dogs away from me. They had stopped barking, but they hadn't moved – they were still growling at me, waiting for her to tell them what to do.

'Please Madam, the dogs will bite me,' I pleaded, not moving my eyes from them.

'No, they won't bite you.' Then she spoke to them nicely, 'Get away now – go on,' and they went off. She was like a doll, her hair almost orange in colour, all curls round her made-up face. Her eyelashes fluttered like a doll's. Her thin lips were bright red like her long nails, and she wore very high-heeled shoes. She was still smiling; I wondered if it didn't hurt after a while. When her friends came for a swim, I could always hear her forever laughing at something or other.

She scared me – I couldn't understand how she could smile like that but not want me to stay in her house.

'When did you come in? We didn't see you.'

'I've been here for some time now – my sister isn't here.

I'm waiting to talk to her.'

'Oh – she's not here?' She was laughing for no reason that I could see. 'I can give her a message – you go on home – I'll tell her that you want to see her.'

Once I was outside the gate, I didn't know what to do or where to go. I walked slowly, kicking my heels. The street lights were so very bright! Like big eyes staring at me. I wondered what the people who saw me thought I was doing, walking around at that time of the night. But then I didn't really care, because there wasn't much I could do about the situation right then. I was just thinking how things had to go wrong on that day particularly, because my sister and I were not on such good terms. Early that morning, when the alarm had gone for me to wake up, I did not jump to turn it off, so my sister got really angry with me. She had gone on about me always leaving it to ring for too long, as if it was set for her, and not for me. And when I went out to wash, I had left the door open a second too long, and that was enough to earn me another scolding.

Every morning I had to wake up straight away, roll my bedding and put it all under the bed where my sister was sleeping. I was not supposed to put on the light although it was still dark. I'd light a candle, and tiptoe my way out with a soap dish and a toothbrush. My clothes were on a hanger on a nail at the back of the door. I'd take the hanger and close the door as quietly as I could. Everything had to be ready set the night before. A washing basin full of cold water was also ready outside the door, put there because the sound of running water and the loud screech the taps made in the morning could wake the white people and they would wonder what my sister was doing up so early. I'd do my everything and be off the premises by five-thirty with my shoes in my bag – I only put them on once I was safely out of the gate. And that gate made such a noise too. Many times I wished I could jump over it and save myself all that sickening careful-careful business!

Thinking about all these things took my mind away from the biting cold of the night and my wet nose, until I saw my sister walking towards me.

'Mholo, what are you doing outside in the street?' she greeted me. I quickly briefed her on what had happened.

'Oh Yehovah! You can be so dumb sometimes! What were you doing inside in the first place? You know you should have waited for me so we could walk in together. Then I could say you were visiting or something. Now, you tell me, what am I supposed to say to them if they see you come in again? Hayi!'

She walked angrily towards the gate, with me hesitantly following her. When she opened the gate, she turned to me with an impatient whisper.

'And now why don't you come in, stupid?'

I mumbled my apologies, and followed her in. By some miracle no one seemed to have noticed us, and we quickly munched a snack of cold chicken and boiled potatoes and drank our tea, hardly on speaking terms. I just wanted to howl like a dog. I wished somebody would come and be my friend, and tell me that I was not useless, and that my sister did not hate me, and tell me that one day I would have a nice place to live ... anything. It would have been really great to have someone my own age to talk to.

But also I knew that my sister was worried for me, she was scared of her employers. If they were to find out that I lived with her, they would fire her, and then we would both be walking up and down the streets. My eleven rand wages wasn't going to help us at all. I don't know how long I lay like that, unable to fall asleep, just wishing and wishing with tears running into my ears.

The next morning I woke up long before the alarm went off, but I just lay there feeling tired and depressed. If there was a way out, I would not have gone to work, but there was this other strong feeling or longing inside me. It was some kind of pain that pushed me to do everything at double speed and run to my toilet. I call it my toilet because that is exactly how I felt about it. It was very rare that I ever saw anybody else go in there in the mornings. It was like they all knew I was using it, and they had to lay off or something.

When I went there, I didn't really expect to find it occupied.

I felt my spirits really lifting as I put on my shoes outside the gate. I made sure that my notebook was in my bag. In my haste I even forgot my lunch box, but it didn't matter. I was walking faster and my feet were feeling lighter all the time. Then I noticed that the door had been painted, and that a new window pane had replaced the old broken one. I smiled to myself as I reached the door. Before long I was sitting on that toilet seat, writing a poem.

Many more mornings saw me sitting there writing. Sometimes it did not need to be a poem; I wrote anything that came into my head – in the same way I would have done if I'd had a friend to talk to. I remember some days when I felt like I was hiding something from my sister. She did not know about my toilet in the park, and she was not in the least interested in my notebook.

Then one morning I wanted to write a story about what had happened at work the day before; the supervisor screaming at me for not calling her when I'd seen the people who stole two dresses at lunch time. I had found it really funny. I had to write about it and I just hoped there were enough pages left in my notebook. It all came back to me, and I was smiling when I reached for the door, but it would-n't open – it was locked!

I think for the first time I accepted that the toilet was not mine after all. ... Slowly I walked over to a bench nearby, watched the early spring sun come up, and wrote my story anyway.

FROM: Anne Oosthuizen (Ed.),
Sometimes When it Rains,
pp. 1–7. 1987. London: Pandora.

3 Academically speaking

The story 'The Toilet' will have taken you into the experiences of another person (Mhlophe's fictional character). You may have identified or empathized with her. When you read literary criticism, your emotions are usually not engaged in the same way as when you read the literary text that the critic is writing about. That's why it sometimes feels strange or alienating to read a discussion of a book or story that you have enjoyed; the discussion may not seem to match your own emotional response. The literary critic, however, is not heartless – he or she is aware of the feelings produced by texts in readers and looks for abstract ways to explain and think about our responses to writing.

Here is a passage adapted from an academic article by Margaret Daymond about women's writing in South Africa in the 1980s. The original version of the article examines several writers and several texts, but at this point discusses 'The Toilet'.

Gender and 'History': 1980s South African women's stories in English

MARGARET DAYMOND

TAKING UP THE NOTE of women's resourcefulness is Mhlophe's protagonist in 'The Toilet', who recounts her own act of choosing a direction in life. This young woman does have a formal education, but when she comes to town to test her opportunities, the first thing she finds is that there is nowhere for her to live. All she can do is hide in the room in a white suburb that her sister, by virtue of working as a domestic servant, is allowed to occupy. When she does find work, it is as unskilled labour in a clothing factory; when she seeks ways of expressing herself, through writing, the only privacy available to her is a toilet in a park.

The echo of Virginia Woolf's 'room of one's own' may not be deliberate, but the story works at first on exactly the same claim: this woman requires and deserves a secure space of her own in order to be her full self. Once this feminist moment has been established, what is really unexpected is the way Mhlophe's conclusion goes beyond it. When her protagonist goes to the toilet – which she has grown to regard as her own room – and finds it locked against her one morning, she does not collapse; she does not even wilt; she accepts that she has had no real claim on the cabin and, as she tells it, she 'walked over to a bench nearby, watched the early spring sun come up, and wrote my story anyway'.

Where does this resourcefulness (as shown by the word 'anyway') come from? Not from others, for the narrator has shown herself in relation only to unsupportive women. Her sister's outlook has been limited by her exploitative employers. The street-wise young women in the factory scorn her for not playing the sexual game of survival as they do. Thus it must be that she draws entirely on resources within herself, but where do they come from? The story asserts, shows and convinces, but it does not explain.

The reader is left feeling that while Mhlophe's ending shows her optimistic personality, it is also a sign of a new certainty of spirit in black women. This has little to do with politics at the level of public campaigns, but everything to do with what was to bring success to such campaigns. It is a long step from a woman's writing a story to a people's attaining freedom. But this glimpse of a woman's spirited choice represents an inner strength which promises an external equivalent.

The freedom to write is what Mhlophe's narrator's choice is primarily about.

ADAPTED FROM: M. J. Daymond
'Gender and "History": 1980s
South African women's stories in English'.
In *Ariel* January 1996, pp. 203–204.

- ✪ Does Margaret Daymond like 'The Toilet'? If so, why? What does she think is the central idea of the story?
- ✪ Do you think Margaret Daymond's ideas about 'The Toilet' are correct? Do you agree or disagree with them? In other words, do you agree with this interpretation of the story?
- ✪ How do you react to the idea that the main character in 'The Toilet' shows 'women's resourcefulness'?
- ✪ Why do you think the writer links the two ideas of 'women' and 'resourcefulness'?
- ✪ Is this a necessary link? Do you think the writer could simply have said 'resourcefulness'?
- ✪ Do you think that 'resourcefulness' is a quality that women have but men do not have?
- ✪ How do you feel about people's habit of linking certain human characteristics (such as caring, kindness, bravery, strength) with specific genders? Are these characteristics necessarily associated with specific genders?

Margaret Daymond also claims elsewhere in her article that people are supplied with 'versions of information about themselves'. This is a useful way of thinking about character, gender, writing and culture. (For instance, the story we created around the characters of Harry and Sally in section two looked at how our assumptions and experiences lead us to believe various things about the roles we should play in specific situations.) You may find the concept of 'versions of information about ourselves' useful as we continue our exploration of concepts of gender in this chapter. It may also prove useful as you study other kinds of discourse° in other chapters.

To summarize the ideas we have discussed in this section, write some kind of text (such as a poem, a lyric for a song, a paragraph, or a speech) in which you explore your own ideas about the concept of being able to escape gender and write. In order to do this, imagine expressing yourself with perfect freedom. What would you say if you felt completely unrestricted?

How does gender limit our freedom?

. . . .

HAS OUR DISCUSSION of gender changed the way you read and think about texts? In this section, we will relate some of what we have been thinking about to extracts from a novel by Jane Austen and a novel by Gabriel Garcia Márquez. We will also explore some aspects of the idea of perspective.

READING STORIES

 Picture perfect

Jane Austen's novel *Pride and Prejudice* (first published in England in 1813) focuses on the development of the relationship between its main female and male characters, Elizabeth Bennett and Mr Darcy. Initially they dislike each other and have mistaken assumptions about each other's values. This obstructs the growth of a happy relationship between them. But such obstacles are overcome and a friendship develops, followed eventually by love and marriage.

At the point in the novel where Elizabeth Bennett becomes aware of how much she is attracted to Mr Darcy, she is reacting to a portrait of him that she is seeing for the first time. She has previously been convinced that she does not completely like him, let alone love him. Her reaction reveals to herself (and to the reader) that in fact she is far more attracted to Darcy than she has thought previously.

N THE *gallery*◇ there were many family *portraits,*◇ but they could have little to fix the attention of a stranger. Elizabeth walked on *in quest of*◇ the only face whose features would be known to her. At last it *arrested*◇ her – and she *beheld a striking resemblance*◇ of Mr Darcy, with such a smile over the face, as she remembered to have sometimes seen when he looked at her. She stood several minutes before the picture in earnest *contemplation,*◇ and returned to it again before they *quitted*◇ the gallery. Mrs Reynolds informed them that it had been taken in his father's lifetime.

There was certainly at this moment in Elizabeth's mind a more gentle *sensation towards the original*◇ than she had ever felt in the height of their acquaintance. The *commendation bestowed on him by Mrs Reynolds was of no trifling nature.*◇ What praise is more valuable than the praise of an intelligent servant? As a brother, a landlord, a master, she considered how many people's happiness were in his *guardianship!, How much of pleasure or pain it was in his power to bestow! – How much of good or evil must be done by him!*◇ Every idea that had been brought forward by the housekeeper was favourable to his character, and as she stood before the canvas on which he was represented, and fixed his eyes upon herself, she *thought of his regard with a deeper sentiment of gratitude than it had ever raised before;*◇ she remembered its warmth, and *softened its impropriety of expression.*◇

FROM: Jane Austen, *Pride and Prejudice* (first published 1813), p. 185. 1981. New York: Bantam.

◇ a room in which art is displayed

◇ she noticed the portrait of Darcy

◇ thinking deeply

◇ she felt sympathy and liking for Darcy

◇ paintings of people

◇ looking for

◇ she saw an amazing similarity between the picture and the real person

◇ left

◇ the praise of Mrs Reynolds was sincere and important

◇ his different roles in his family and society make him very powerful over people

◇ she felt more grateful for the fact that he liked her

◇ she was now more forgiving of what had irritated her in Darcy's behaviour

MADE FOR EACH OTHER

When I read this with a sense that gender is significant for the way stories are created, I find myself thinking about Elizabeth's reaction to Darcy's portrait. What strikes me is that she is reacting strongly to a representation of Darcy which shows him in terms of male and class power. In other words, in his portrait Darcy becomes a symbol of power. Firstly, he is a wealthy landlord who is represented as a generous ruler. This is shown by the information we are given that he has 'many people's happiness ... in his guardianship', and that he is admired by his employee Mrs Reynolds.

Secondly, the portrait also shows Darcy, in the way Elizabeth interprets the picture, as an example of good maleness. She sees him, admiringly, as 'a brother, a landlord, a master'. Images of him as a good person cannot be separated from images of his various male roles. In an important way, her falling in love seems to be catalysed (caused) by an attraction to what he represents. Elizabeth sees in him her own idea of good male qualities. She is attracted to him because he seems to have what she thinks of as the qualities and characteristics of a good man.

2 Telling it like it might be

One of the ideas explored in Gabriel Garcia Márquez's novel *Chronicle of a Death Foretold* is how assumptions about gender affect the ways people act. The plot or narrative scheme of this book occurs in the form of a hunt for the truth. The narrator is like a detective or a reporter and the narrative is similar to the kind used in detective novels. The narrator tries to solve the mystery of a murder. At least, he tries to solve the mystery of exactly why the victim was murdered. He tries to reconstruct the events leading up to the murder of one of the characters, Santiago Nassar.

The events described in the novel occur in a small town in Colombia, South America. This is the setting, or context, of the narrative. The novel presents the accounts of various people, those involved in the murder and those who witnessed it. The murderers of Santiago Nassar are known, in fact the murder was committed in public and the culprits admitted their responsibility and were convicted and imprisoned.

Nevertheless, there is still debate and controversy about important aspects of the case many years after the murder. The major question is whether or not Santiago Nassar was 'guilty' of the behaviour that led the Vicario brothers to kill him, for his murder is a revenge killing. The brothers' sister, Angela Vicario, marries on the day before the murder. But her husband rejects her on their wedding night when she informs him that she is not a virgin. She claims to her angry family, when they question her, that Santiago Nassar has been her lover. In order to 'avenge the family's honour', her brothers kill him.

This novel is interesting in many ways. One thing it does is question assumptions about honour in relation to gender. The community in which the events occur believes in concepts of machismo and an 'honour code'. These concepts of honour and machismo are based on ideas of appropriate male and female behaviour.

> **machismo** /mə'tʃɪzməʊ; *US* mɑː'tʃiːz-/ *n* [U] (*usu derog*) aggressive pride in being male: *He combines Hollywood charisma with cowboy machismo.*
>
> **mach·is·mo** /£mɔ'kɪz·məʊ, $-moʊ/ *n* [U] *often disapproving* strong pride in behaving in a fierce and forceful way which is thought to be typically male •

However, what becomes clear in the book is that these concepts can all be questioned and seem to have no final or absolute truth. As the story unfolds, they seem less and less real and more and more open to being questioned. It becomes clear that there is no consistency among the reports. Everyone has a different idea of what happened, when it happened, and what made people act as they did. The stories told vary from witness to witness, so that certainty becomes uncertainty – from the weather on the day of the murder, to the actions of the characters, to the order in which the actions occurred. What emerges is that the events and people's ideas about them and about one another are all dependent on events which may or may not have occurred. They depend on context and possibility, not necessity.

The unreliability of evidence about simple physical details invites the reader to question all aspects of the narrative. This questioning includes a questioning of the beliefs and codes according to which people act. All the characters have versions of themselves (to pick up on a phrase we mentioned earlier) on which they see themselves as needing to act. However, the versions of themselves which they present, and their perceptions of others, become completely unreliable.

Think about the following extract from *Chronicle of a Death Foretold*. What ideas about gender does it express or suggest? The extract refers to Angela Vicario, the woman who is rejected by her husband for not being a virgin when they marry. She is described here many years after her failed marriage. She has revealed that she has not lived with her husband, but has written many letters to him.

ER LIFE AS A REJECTED WIFE continued on, simple as that of an old maid, still doing machine embroidery with her friends, just as before she had made cloth tulips and paper birds, but when her mother went to bed she would stay in the room until dawn writing letters with no future. She became lucid, overbearing, mistress of her own free will, and she became a virgin again just for him, and she recognized no other authority than her own ...

FROM: Gabriel Garcia Márquez, *Chronicle of a Death Foretold*, p. 94. Translated by Gregory Rabassa. 1982. London: Penguin.

One thing that we notice about the description of Angela Vicario here is that perspective or point of view affects people's ideas of themselves and of each other. Angela Vicario re-makes her own idea of herself, and this affects other people's ideas about her. She is able to see herself as strong and in charge of her own life – in fact, she can see herself as a virgin and can make others see her as that too. She rejects other ideas that people hold about her. In a sense, she has different identities, depending on whose perspective she is seen from. From her mother's perspective, she is a rejected wife, an old maid with no power or independence. From her own perspective she is strong and in charge of her own life and identity. This is the image of herself she makes and presents when she writes to her husband. What this demonstrates is that perspective, or point of view, determines the way people, objects and events are seen. Defining people in terms of categories (such as gender categories) is ultimately a matter of perception – of how we see each other. Often, how we see people depends on the images we create of them or the representations we construct.

· ·

FIVE

CREATING COMPARATIVE WRITING

The first two chapters of this book have explored kinds of writing which encourage a personal response – the writing of autobiography and the characterization of other people. In this section, we will look at a slightly more abstract skill: comparative writing.

Comparison is a skill which forms the basis of much thinking and formal study. In your studies, you may often be asked to compare two or more things (two novels, for example, or the behaviour of characters in texts). When we compare things, we look for the similarities and differences between them.

Let's look at the following traditional rhyme to start thinking about the requirements of comparative writing.

What are little boys made of?
What are little boys made of?
Frogs and snails
And puppy dogs' tails,
That's what little boys are made of.

What are little girls made of?
What are little girls made of?
Sugar and spice
And all that's nice,
That's what little girls are made of.

How do you feel about the way this rhyme describes 'little boys' and 'little girls'? What does the rhyme say about femininity and masculinity?

The rhyme compares boys and girls by characterizing them in stereotypes. It follows a common pattern of comparison by first presenting ideas about one aspect of the two things being compared, and then giving ideas about the second one. This pattern of writing could be simply expressed as follows:

Item 1 – qualities Item 2 – qualities

Let's call this 'STRUCTURE A'.

However, comparisons are frequently structured in other ways too, like this, for instance:

Quality 1 of Items 1 and 2
Quality 2 of Items 1 and 2
Quality 3 of Items 1 and 2
Quality 4 of Items 1 and 2
Quality 5 ... etc.

We will call this 'STRUCTURE B'.

The rhyme quoted above clearly uses STRUCTURE A. If we were to re-write it as a short paragraph we could end up with something like this:

Little boys are made of various objectionable things. They are created from frogs, snails and puppy dogs' tails. On the other hand, little girls are made of pleasant things such as sugar and spice and all that's nice. That's what little girls are made of.

Re-writing the rhyme using STRUCTURE B would give us this:

Little boys are made of frogs and snails, but little girls consist of sugar and spice. Puppy dogs' tails also go into making little boys, whereas little girls are made of all that's nice. As you can see, little boys are made up from various objectionable things while little girls are made of pleasant things.

USEFUL WORDS FOR COMPARISON AND CONTRAST

When you are writing comparisons and contrasts, you may find it useful to use signpost words to mark the transition between one point and the next. Some of these signpost words are:

on the one hand ... on the other hand
similarly   in the same way
but   nevertheless
however   by contrast
unlike

Both structures have weaknesses. The problem with STRUCTURE A is that the comparison might not emerge clearly enough from what you write. Completing the description of one thing before moving on to the next may not help your reader to see the similarities and differences easily. On the other hand, if you decide to use STRUCTURE B, in which you compare corresponding qualities of each thing in isolation, it may become difficult to focus clearly on the larger picture. Your reader might become distracted by thinking about the details and lose track of the main point that you are trying to make.

Comparing two or more things involves more than describing the items separately, although description is part of it. Before writing a piece of comparative writing, make a list of the qualities of each thing you are going to compare. Then list the important similarities and differences between the items you are comparing. These lists will help you to focus on what seems important about the items for the purposes of comparison. At this point, you will also be able to decide what structure to use for your writing: would STRUCTURE A or STRUCTURE B be the best choice? Your decision will depend on your own feelings about what would be the most effective way to convey your ideas.

Here are some exercises in comparison. For each exercise, make short notes and list whatever similarities and differences you see.

Then decide, by looking at your lists, how you would structure a piece of writing on each topic.

✪ Compare how you see yourself with how you think people see you.
✪ Compare what your life is like with what you dream it could be like.

TIME OFF
TO WRITE!

In chapter two we discussed Can Themba's short story 'The Suit' in order to look at various ideas about characterization and writing. However, we did not specifically explore ways of thinking about it in terms of gender. As you worked through this chapter, though, you might have found yourself thinking about 'The Suit' as you reflected on ideas about texts and gender. Whether you did or not, think back to 'The Suit' bearing in mind the ideas about gender we have looked at in this chapter.

✪ What ideas do you think Philemon has about masculinity and femininity (that is, gender)?
✪ What ideas do you think Matilda has about masculinity and femininity?
✪ Re-read the story. Make notes about the ideas Matilda and Philemon seem to have about gender. As you make these notes, take care to indicate what evidence there is that they hold these ideas. You should be able to link any claim you make about what they think to what they do and say. You might quote descriptions of events or of speech directly from the text, or you might refer to things that occur in the story. These notes are an important step in the process of producing a piece of writing about a text, since they will help you to support what you say about it.
✪ Now produce a piece of writing (of at least one page) in which you compare and contrast Philemon's and Matilda's ideas about what is appropriate for men and women.

4 Writing Worlds Apart: Representing Cultures

THIS BOOK HAS DISCUSSED how we describe ourselves and other individuals in language and how gender is represented in texts. What we will be examining in this chapter are the various ways in which unfamiliar or different cultures are represented in speech and writing. We will think about how perspective relates to the idea of 'culture' and consider some of the difficulties involved in writing about groups of people. Our focus will be on the representation of other people, particularly in the context of colonialism and imperialism. This chapter should help you develop your own ideas about how the language we use to represent people, things and ideas reveals what we think about them.

. . . .

1 Perceptions and reactions

WE HAVE ALREADY been introduced to the idea that we always look from somewhere. This idea might seem obvious. Often, though, we forget that we are situated in a particular world (or context). We forget that our understanding of things in the world is affected by where we are from. If you were to describe a society other than your own, your description would be affected by the difference between your world and the world you are observing and describing. How you will describe something depends on where you come from and what you are speaking or writing about. There is no such thing as a description entirely unaffected by an author's attitudes, beliefs and the society from which she or he comes.

Think back to chapter one, which explored concepts of the self and autobiographical writing. That chapter may have left you with a strong sense of who you are (or the many ways in which you exist in the world) and of the world from which you come. Think now of your encounters with worlds different from your own. Think about your own experience of different worlds before we look at the experiences of other people. Have you ever moved into a new work or social environment where things seemed strange and different to you?

✪ How did you feel at first?

✪ How did you act?

✪ What did you do to try to understand the new things you encountered?

✪ Did you make any mistakes?

✪ Did you adapt? How?

Have you met people (perhaps from another country) whose culture differs from your own?

✪ What made that culture seem different from others?

✪ How did you react to members of that culture?

✪ How did you feel about members of that culture?

✪ Did you consider that culture to be equal to your own?

✪ Did you want to understand more about that culture?

The City of Despina

THE COASTAL CITY OF DESPINA CAN BE REACHED in two ways: by ship or by camel. The city looks different to the traveller arriving overland than it looks to him who arrives by sea.

When the camel-driver arriving at Despina from the desert sees, on the horizon, the buildings of Despina, the chimneys smoking, the windsocks flapping, he thinks of a ship: he knows that it is a city, but he thinks of it as a ship that will take him away from the desert. He sees the city as a ship that is about to leave harbour, the breeze already filling its sails. He thinks of all the foreign ports to which the ship might take him, of all the foreign merchandise that cranes are unloading on docks. He dreams of the chance to drink in bars in exciting places and of witnessing the fights and arguments between men from different countries. He thinks too of the possibility of meeting exotic women.

The sailor, approaching Despina from the sea, sees in the city's shape the form of a camel advancing into the desert. The camel has an embroidered saddle with a glittering fringe and is swaying gently as it moves towards oases in the middle of the desert. The sailor knows that Despina is a city, but he thinks of it as a camel with wineskins hanging from its pack and carrying bundles of wonderful food. He pictures himself as being at the front of a caravan moving away from the sea towards the shade and fresh water of an oasis filled with palm trees. He imagines the white-walled buildings of the oasis, each surrounding a courtyard in which beautiful women dance barefoot, half-hidden by veils of silk.

Each city is seen and understood differently depending on where you approach it from. The sailor and the camel-driver see, in the shape of Despina, something that will take them away from what is familiar to something new and exciting. For this reason, Despina is a border city between two deserts.

ADAPTED FROM: Italo Calvino, *Invisible Cities*, pp. 17–18, 1979. London: Pan Books.

Despina is an imaginary city created by the Italian author, Italo Calvino. His description of the ways in which the sailor and camel-driver see the city makes an interesting point about how we see things. We can never see reality just *as it is*. Different people see things in different ways. Any act of seeing is an interpretation°: a process° of giving meaning to what we see. Both the sailor and the camel-driver give the city a particular meaning.

They interpret the city in different ways by seeing in it particular possibilities that define the city *for them*.

✪ How can we account for the fact that the camel-driver and the sailor see different 'things' when looking at Despina?

The answer to this question should help us find an answer to the following:
✪ What makes us see the world in the way we do?

As we have discussed earlier, 'perspective' refers to the place from which we look at things. The sailor and camel-driver are both looking at the same thing (the city) but they see it from different spatial perspectives: one from the sea and one from the desert. But it is not only their spatial perspectives that affect their interpretations of the city. What makes them understand the city differently is their situation. The sailor might have spent many months at sea and so interprets the city as a chance to experience things he desires and has missed while away.

Similarly, the camel-driver connects the city with the things he has missed most in the desert. They arrive at the city from different worlds (the sea and the desert) and interpret the city's appearance in terms of where they have come from and what they have experienced.

The concept of 'perspective' refers to far more than our physical location when looking at something. It suggests that the way we see things in the world relates to the place from which we look, but that 'place' is not only a physical location. 'Place' also refers to our state of mind and our expectations. In this sense, our perspective is created largely by the world in which we have grown up and in which we have learnt certain ways of seeing. These social factors combine with our individual choices to form the particular situation in which each of us lives.

In the previous chapters we considered how we live in complex contexts made up of everything that forms our world. Gender, race, occupation, social rituals, lifestyle, language, religious faith, economic class, political beliefs, educational background, family relationships and our environment all influence our perceptions. What we see and how we understand or interpret the world around us depends on both what we are looking at and the context from within which we look.

One of the most important factors that affects how we see and interpret the world is the culture from which we come. We have used the word 'culture' at times in this book before, but we need to discuss this concept in more detail. If we assume that all members of a culture think or behave in exactly the same way, our assumption would be factually inaccurate and racist (a concept we will discuss at length later). However, we do need to establish what cultural difference is and how it affects our understanding of (and behaviour in) the world.

2 Culture

WHAT IS 'CULTURE'?

The word 'culture' is used in so many ways in our society.
✪ Have you ever heard the word 'culture' used in discussions?
✪ What does the word describe?
✪ What do you, therefore, understand by the word 'culture'?
✪ Write down the best definition of 'culture' that you can and then compare it with this definition from the *Oxford Advanced Learner's Dictionary*.

● HAVE you omitted anything from your definition? Do you feel the dictionary overlooks anything?

culture /ˈkʌltʃə(r)/ *n* **1** [U] (**a**) art, literature, music and other intellectual expressions of a particular society or time: *a society without much culture* ∘ *a period of high/low culture* ∘ *Universities should be centres of culture.* (**b**) an understanding or appreciation of this: *She is a woman of considerable culture.* (**c**) (*often derog*) art, literature, etc in general: *tourists coming to Venice in search of culture.* **2** [C, U] the customs, arts, social institutions, etc of a particular group or nation: *people from different cultures* ∘ *Western culture* ∘ *working-class culture* ∘ *twentieth-century popular culture.* **3** [U] development through regular training, exercise, treatment, etc: *physical culture* (ie becoming fit and strong by doing exercises) ∘ *The culture of the mind is vital.* **4** [U] the growing of plants or breeding of certain types of animal to obtain a crop or improve the species: *the culture of bees/silkworms.* **5** [C] (*biology*) a group of bacteria grown for medical or scientific study: *a culture of cholera germs.*

'Culture' has been described as 'one of the two or three most complicated words in the English language' (Raymond Williams, *Keywords*, p. 87. 1983. London: Fontana). It is a complicated word because it has a complex history and is used in very different ways. The earliest recorded use of the word (in the early sixteenth century) referred to a society's cultivating practices. In other words, 'culture' referred to whether a society grew crops, raised animals or was nomadic.

The word now suggests the fact that societies in different places, and at different times, are organized differently. Societies have different social, political and religious systems which they perform in different ways. But in spite of these differences, there are important similarities between societies. No culture exists free of the influence of other cultures, even when governments (such as those of North Korea or contemporary China, for example) attempt to achieve this. In the modern world, technologically advanced countries are able to spread their influence (and products) throughout most societies, affecting the culture of those societies. It is important, therefore, to think of cultures as ever-changing entities under constant influence from other cultures.

There is a second, less commonly used sense of the word 'culture'. In this sense, 'culture' means the same as 'civilization'. When used in this way, 'culture' refers to the level of development of a society; in other words, 'cultured' societies are those that have reached an advanced state of intellectual and artistic activity. Similarly, the word is also used to describe an individual whose tastes are sophisticated (someone who likes art, literature, good food and classical music might be described as 'cultured').

Imagine you are confronted with two separate groups of people. Look at the following pictures and then complete the task that follows. You'll have to use your imagination and think carefully about the pictures.

GROUP 1   GROUP 2

The individuals in GROUP 1 work in a modern city. They drive expensive motor cars, all own cellphones and all work in tertiary service industries (as lawyers, accountants, doctors, consultants, politicians). Most of the group see themselves as 'cultured' in the second sense of the word discussed above: they visit cinemas, theatres, classical music performances and expensive restaurants. Most of them work on computers and most live in houses with television sets, video recorders and alarm systems.

GROUP 2 is made up of a community of mystics who live in a remote part of a large Eastern country. Their community has not adopted (and could not afford) the technology that GROUP 1 takes for granted. They live according to the same principles and have the same lifestyle that their community has embodied for the last thousand years. This community trades according to the barter system: what they manufacture or grow they trade (or swop) with neighbouring communities. Their priorities are spiritual: the most important people in the community are those who have come closest to the ideals of spirituality.

Your task is to do the following. Imagine an argument between two people who are talking about GROUPS 1 and 2. One person is arguing that GROUP 1 is more 'advanced' than GROUP 2 and the other is disagreeing with her.

✪ List five arguments that could be used in support of the idea that GROUP 1 is more advanced than GROUP 2.

✪ How could these arguments be opposed?

As you have discovered from doing this exercise, the question of whether one society is more or less advanced than another is a complex one. Defining 'advanced' is not easy. Similarly, societies often have their own definitions of progress and development. Progress is not only a matter of technological development. This assumption is a very narrow understanding of what progress might be. As will become clearer later in this section, whether societies are seen as advanced or not is often what determines how they are treated by other societies.

We will be looking at the ways in which cultures present themselves as more advanced than (and, therefore, superior to) other cultures. We will also be looking at the consequences that this belief can have.

Most contemporary writers avoid making any judgements about the extent to which societies are 'developed'. Often such a judgement would not be relevant to their purposes and, in any case, the level of 'development' could only be determined by judging one culture by the standards of another. You will often encounter the word 'culture' in the phrases 'cultural context' and 'cultural difference'. These phrases are based on the assumption that our cultural context is relevant to the way that we interpret the world and that cultures differ in important ways. These phrases, when we use them in discussion, are not evaluative claims: they are never assertions that one society is better or worse than another.

The fact that much of this chapter deals with cultures rather than individuals does not mean that:

- ✪ all individuals in a particular culture see things in exactly the same way;
- ✪ cultures cannot be closely connected or that one culture cannot be deeply influenced by another;
- ✪ everyone feels the same about the culture to which he or she belongs; and
- ✪ it is impossible for you to challenge the cultural context from which you come.

HUNTERS AND GATHERERS

It is often assumed from a Western, technological perspective that hunter-gatherer communities – where people survive by utilizing the food sources that they can find in their environment – are inherently 'primitive' or 'uncivilized'. Anthropologists (scholars who study different societies or cultures) have realized that these societies are highly structured and are governed by complex belief and value systems. Let's look at a single example of a social practice in a hunting and gathering society, the Khoisan of the Kalahari Desert.

Hunting in Khoisan society happens in groups of three or four hunters. However, the meat is divided up not just among the hunters and their families, but among the entire band (or social group). The main responsibility for the division rests with the owner of the first arrow responsible for killing the animal. The owner of the first arrow is not necessarily the hunter who shoots the arrow. An intricate system of lending and borrowing arrows in Khoisan society ensures a fair distribution of meat throughout the society. Such a form of food distribution seems both more humane and efficient than the situation found in many so-called 'developed' societies, where people without the means to generate an income may starve to death.

WRITING WORLDS APART

In a multi-cultural context like South Africa there is often a tension between preserving the cultural identities of different groups (whether they are based on religion, race or language) and promoting national unity. Obviously it is essential to encourage tolerance and dialogue. But how far should society go?

✪ To what extent do you think the cultural identities of different groups deserve to be protected?

✪ Is there a danger in arguing that cultures are distinct and separate in a context where people live and work closely alongside one another?

✪ Should we attempt to throw all cultures into a 'melting pot' so that they merge into a single national culture?

✪ To what extent do you feel an individual is defined by the culture of which she or he is a member?

WHAT IS YOUR CULTURE?

At those points where cultures collide with one another or inter-act, it is very difficult to separate individuals from their context. When two or more cultures come into contact with one another we often become aware of the differences between them as well as of their similarities. One reason for this could be that when we are confronted with another culture, we become representatives of our own culture. Outside of our own culture, we are often taken as representing, in some direct sense, the entire culture of which we are a member. We are, unquestionably, more aware of the fact of culture when we find ourselves at the borders of our own and other cultures.

Imagine that you have just returned from a visit to Botswana, where you have encountered Tswana culture. You visited a series of villages, saw the democratic kgotla system in operation (which gives adults the right to argue in public before decisions are made by local authorities) and were impressed by the art and educational practices of the society. You decide that you wish to become a Motswana and wish to live a life as close to that of the villagers of western Botswana as possible. Assuming that you are not a Motswana or Mosotho, you would have to learn the language and learn more about the culture. Imagine that you do so, that you emigrate and find yourself in a remote Botswana village.

✪ To what degree do you think you would be accepted by the local people?

✪ Imagine that you are visited by people from your own earlier culture. How might they respond to the changes you have made?

✪ Would you still 'feel' as if you are a member of your culture 'back home'?

✪ How much of your culture would you forget?

✪ Could you simply return to your own culture?

Clearly, not everyone will answer these questions in the same way. The cultural changes that the transition would demand of a Japanese student from Kyoto, for instance, would be entirely different to those demanded of a Setswana-speaking student from the Northern Province of South Africa.

TIME OFF
TO TALK!

Discuss this question below with someone you know.

✪ Can individuals leave one culture to join another?
If this is possible, how would they go about doing so?

If a person wanted to move from one culture to another successfully (rather than just visit it as an outsider), she or he would most probably have to:

✪ learn the language of the society;

✪ attempt to follow its social, religious and political practices;

✪ respect the people's beliefs; and

✪ accept the forms of authority in the society as valid.

It is difficult to say whether these conditions can ever be met. Some anthropologists have tried to get inside the communities they are studying by becoming 'one of the people' in the culture. Their reasons for trying to do this have, however, been questioned. It is also highly debatable whether their attempts have in fact been successful.

THE DANGERS OF 'CULTURE'

Are there any dangers in speaking of 'culture' as it relates to the ways we see the world? As soon as we speak of cultures as unified and coherent, or substitute a stereotype for the complex nature of any society, we run the risk of racism. If we asserted that all individuals in a culture see things in a certain way, we would be generalizing. Most societies have considerable variations within them and we would need to bear this in mind. Individuals within a society may differ from one another more than they differ from individuals in other societies. Furthermore, no individual sees the world purely through the eyes of his or her culture. Our own unique experiences, choices, circumstances and preferences all affect the way that we see and understand our world.

Think about yourself and about a friend or relative who belongs to the same culture as you, and answer these questions:
- Do you listen to the same music?
- Do you have the same taste in clothing?
- Do you have the same attitude to sport?
- Do you like the same foods and drink the same drinks?
- Do you always agree with each other about matters of political and religious belief?
- If you are both married, do you treat your spouses in exactly the same way?

Your answers to these questions will probably leave you with the conclusion that being from the same culture does not mean that you are exactly the same. This is true of people in all cultural groups.

Why, then, do we speak of 'cultures' at all? At various points in the history of humankind, cultures have come into contact with one another. At the point of meeting, individuals develop ways of understanding and describing the culture they encounter. Through descriptions of other cultures they are also defining and defending (or criticizing) their own culture. These descriptions, which we will call representations of cultures, are very important because they affect the ways in which members of different cultures behave towards one another. Without answering the question of whether cultural difference is in fact very important, the truth is that throughout history people have lived with the idea of cultural difference and have behaved on the basis of their understanding of it.

Our language: our world

OTHERS AND 'OTHERS'

Arising out of literary theory are the terms 'others' and 'the other' (or 'the Other'). These terms convey the idea that groups in society create an identity for themselves through defining themselves as different from other cultures, or even as different from groups within their own culture. One way to understand a group's cultural identity (who they consider themselves to be), is to identify who they think they are not. In other words, that group's ideas about how they differ from others tell us a great deal about how they think about themselves.

Having considered some ideas about 'cultural context' and 'cultural difference', we need to look at the relationship between language and culture. Because most representations of cultures are expressed in language (though also in film and the visual arts), we need to consider the significance of language to culture and to the process of representation. Write down answers to the following questions, since it would be useful if your own ideas on the matter are clear before you encounter the ideas of other people.

✪ Do different cultures necessarily speak different languages?
✪ Do we define different cultures on the basis of the languages they speak?
✪ Can dialogue occur between members of different cultures? If so, how?
✪ Is it possible to translate completely accurately from one language to another, especially where obvious cultural differences exist?
✪ Do all languages name the same things?
✪ Do languages contain within them the culture of their speakers?

Have you ever heard someone who speaks more than one language say, 'There are words in one language that don't have exact equivalents in another language'? An example is the word 'computer' in English. In Japanese, in which there was no word to express the idea, the word sounds like 'co-poo-ta-ra', which comes from the way some pronounce the English word. In English we have a concept we refer to with the word 'weekdays'; in Italian there is no single word for this concept. Instead, it is represented by the phrase '*Lunedi a Venerdi*', which literally means 'Monday to

Friday'. There are also examples from South Africa, such as the Sotho 'teye' (pronounced 'ti-ya') for the English word 'tea'. The English word was, in a sense, 'Sotho-ized' or modified to fit the grammar and pronunciation of Sesotho.

Let's think back to our question about whether we can translate completely accurately between languages. Translation is a more complex process than merely looking for a word in one language that means exactly the same as a word in another. An extreme point of view concerning translation would maintain that precise translation from one language to another is not in any real sense possible. Some linguists have suggested that the structure of people's language might influence the way they see the world and name things within it. Other scholars, however, hold that culture shapes the grammar and vocabulary of a language. Whatever we might feel about this debate, the fact remains that all languages describe the world somewhat differently.

Even though direct translation from one language into another might not always seem possible, we all know that most concepts expressed in one language can be translated into another. Often, it might be necessary to use more words in the translation than in the original version in order to convey the meaning more fully. Concepts can also be created in the act of translation even if they do not exist in the language to start with. This suggests that there is a large degree of similarity in the way that different languages provide concepts through which we interpret the world.

Why all these questions about the possibility of translation? Languages, because they do name different concepts, indicate that thought about the world and the language through which we describe it cannot be separated. The debate about whether the language we speak determines what we think or whether we think things and then find names for them is an ongoing and interesting one. We will certainly not try to solve the problem here. But if we consider the difficulties of translation, we can draw the following conclusions.

✪ There is an important connection between the language we speak and how we interpret the world.

✪ Language names things and concepts and could shape how we think about the world.

IN HIS NOVEL *Things Fall Apart*, the Nigerian author Chinua Achebe does not attempt to translate certain words from the Ibo language. The novel describes the Ibo society as it existed in the Niger Delta in the last years of the eighteenth century.

One word that Achebe does not translate is *osu*. In the glossary in the text, Achebe defines *osu* as 'outcast; having been dedicated to a god, the *osu* was taboo, and was not allowed to mix with the freeborn in any way.' (Chinua Achebe, *Things Fall Apart*, p.150. 1958. London: Heinemann) The *osu* were a group of individuals divided from Ibo society yet still members of it, who had been given by the tribe as a gift to a god. Non-*osu* (freeborn) Ibo did not associate with the *osu*: they would not converse, eat or share accommodation with the *osu*.

The word names a cultural/religious practice of the Ibo people. The word '*osu*' cannot be translated into English except through a complex description of the practice itself. An Ibo tribesman might think of people as being either *osu* or freeborn: the concept is part of his way of interpreting the people around him. When an Ibo tribesman comes to talk to a speaker of another language, say English, he will have to translate the idea *osu* into terms that an English speaker would understand.

The English words 'outcast' (Oxford Advanced Learner's Dictionary: 'a person who is driven away from home, friends or society, or who has no place in society') and 'taboo' ('a cultural or religious custom that forbids people to do, touch, use or talk about a certain thing: "the taboo against incest"; "tribal taboos"; "Death is one of the great taboos in our culture"') can be used in conjunction to explain the word *osu*, but they do not express the full significance of the word in Ibo culture. The word reflects a particular belief or way of seeing the world. Its existence reflects an aspect of Ibo culture and any attempt to translate it into another language will involve representing the practice in the terms of another language.

✪ Cross-cultural communication is a complex, but important, process to understand.

✪ If we describe another culture in our own language, we are describing it in our own terms.

✪ Our language both reflects and creates our cultural context, because we behave in the world in accordance with the way that we represent it in language.

④ Two ways in which words mean

One of the ways that we attempt to understand a culture is by looking at how language reflects certain methods of understanding and describing the world. Because this section is particularly concerned with the ways in which people represent other cultures in language, we need to look at some of the questions surrounding meaning in language.

Two terms that are useful when we discuss what a word means are denotation° and connotation°. Denotation refers to the main meaning of a word, the one usually supplied first in a dictionary definition. Connotation, however, is a little more tricky: it refers to the ideas we associate with a word. So the word 'bee' denotes, according to the Oxford Advanced Learner's Dictionary, 'an insect with four wings that can sting'. This description is quite clear, but it doesn't quite cover all the things we imagine when we think of a bee. The word 'bee' carries with it connotations of, for example, hard work and determination. We use some of the connotations of 'bee' when we use it in the phrase, 'as busy as a bee'.

The connotations we associate with a word can be created by the time and place in which we live. For example, in the United States of America, the word 'township' doesn't have particularly strong connotations; the word denotes, quite simply, 'a town, or town and the area around it, that has certain powers of local government'. In South Africa, 'township' denotes 'a town where mainly black citizens live'. An American would not associate many different connotations with the word, but a South African certainly would: connotations of poverty, apartheid, struggle and township jazz are just some that spring to mind.

THE WAR OF WORDS

Language is seldom neutral, especially in times of war.
Think about the implications of the following comparisons:

we have	**they have**
an army, navy, air force	a war machine
reporting guidelines	censorship
press briefings	propaganda
we	**they**
take out	destroy
suppress	kill, neutralize or eliminate
dig in	cower in their foxholes
we launch	**they launch**
first strikes pre-emptively	sneak missile attacks without provocation
our men are	**their men are**
boys	troops
lads	hordes

our boys are	theirs are
professional	brainwashed
lion-hearted	paper tigers
cautious	cowardly
confident	desperate
heroes	cornered
dare-devils	cannon fodder
loyal	blindly obedient
resolute	ruthless
brave	fanatical

our boys	their boys
fly into the jaws of hell	cower in concrete bunkers

our missiles cause	their missiles cause
collateral damage	civilian casualties

we	they
precision-bomb	fire wildly at anything in the sky

our leader is	their leader is
at peace with himself	demented
resolute	defiant
statesmanlike	an evil tyrant
assured	a crackpot monster

ADAPTED FROM: Hilary Janks, *Language, identity and power*. 1993. Johannesburg: Hodder & Stoughton in association with the Witwatersrand University Press.

The connotations of words differ widely between individuals and cultures. Certain words evoke associations particular to a culture. Our individual beliefs and opinions also affect the associations a word has for us.

While we can usually translate denotations of words, connotations are difficult if not impossible to translate. Accordingly, when we encounter other cultures, we might understand the denotations of the words they use, but not the full range of connotations. Moreover, when we represent other cultures we use words with particular denotations and connotations. We cannot, therefore, understand cross-cultural communication and representations without thinking in terms of the denotations and connotations of words.

. . . .

THIS SECTION TAKES YOU on a voyage of exploration and asks you to write about (and reflect on) your experiences.

IN A STRANGE LAND

 1   A first encounter

Imagine what it would be like to be in the following situation:

Y OU LIVE FAR IN THE FUTURE, in a time when space travel has become routine. Airports have given way to spaceports and the sight of spacecraft shooting up through the earth's atmosphere is as common as the sight of aircraft was in the twentieth-century. Your heroes are the great explorers of space who have ventured into uncharted galaxies and returned with stories of strange planets and exotic creatures.

Motivated by your fantasies of space travel, you have taken a job in a large mining company which regularly sends missions to the outer reaches of the known universe in pursuit of the mineral wealth of other planets.

For the first three years of your employment by The Company, you work at a desk, becoming increasingly frustrated by typing up and filing the reports lodged by the commanders of spaceships and their crews. You become more and more envious of their adventures and begin to feel quite disgruntled at The Company's failure to allow you to fulfil your ambition.

One morning your chance comes. The commander of one of The Company's space ships arrives at Headquarters. He reports that one of his crew members has fallen seriously ill and he requires a replacement. He needs a competent writer who will keep records on a voyage of discovery to a far-flung galaxy and then write reports for The Directors of The Company. Your superiors agree to let you go on the mission, to do this job. You will be the official observer and record-keeper. You are, of course, delighted at the opportunity, and spend the next week packing and repacking your bag in anticipation. Finally the day to depart arrives.

You have been travelling through space for months. You have seen and heard nothing out of the ordinary, but are continually mesmerized by the beauty of the stars slowly drifting past. There is occasional communication with other spaceships belonging to The Company and with craft piloted by strange creatures from other planets. This is the first time you have actually heard aliens and your imagination runs wild.

Then one day, six months after leaving Earth, something odd happens. The radio engineer on the flight deck of your spacecraft announces that he has picked up a radio signal from a source which does not appear on any of the maps or charts. Something out there, never before encountered by humankind, is sending a signal. The Commander decides to investigate, since his orders are to find new planets which may offer the possibility of mining operations. As your ship approaches the source of the signal, it grows stronger and stronger. Eventually a small blue planet comes into view.

Your ship orbits the planet and a conference is called by the Commander. He, the radio engineer and the ship's linguist are all unable to decode the message in any way, even when using the most sophisticated reading techniques programmed into the onboard computer. It is possible for them, though, to deduce that the message must come from a developed society: primitive messages are always easier to decode.

Because there are no means of communicating with the aliens before attempting to land on their planet, a decision is made to arm a small party, land the ship on the surface of the blue planet and send the party to see what it can find out. Your importance as the official observer and writer makes it essential that you be a member of the exploring party.

———————

The impact of the ship hitting the surface startles you. For so long you have been drifting in the quietness of space: suddenly, for the first time in six months, you are on solid ground. Just as you and the rest of the party are about to don breathing apparatus, the environmental engineer announces that it will not be needed. She has run tests and, much to her amazement, has discovered that the blue planet has a gravitational field very close to that of Earth and a virtually identical atmosphere. She points out that the atmospheric temperature is hot, but will not be unbearably so. It is the hot, dry heat that hits you first as the hatch of your spacecraft opens and you descend the steps. You and the other eleven members of the party are the first humans ever to set foot on the planet.

You stand and stare, amazed. All your life you have longed for this chance: to explore a strange, wonderful and exotic planet. You begin to make a mental list of details that you will include in your report to The Directors. The planet has no vegetation: the sand stretches off into the distance, here and there gathered into small dunes, but what amazes you is how flat this sector of the planet is, how comparatively featureless.

What distinguishes this landscape from the flattest deserts on Earth is the colour of the sand. The planet appeared blue from space not because, as you suspected, it is covered with water, but because the sands of its desert landscape are a rich blue in colour. You look up into the far distance, scanning the horizon. Your observation is interrupted when you notice a large square silver shape. You lift your binoculars and draw the attention of your comrades to the shape you can only just discern through the heat's haze.

Through the binoculars you can make out that the shape is some form of metallic construction. At the foot of the large edifice you can see movement: figures, although you can make out little detail at this range, seem to be scurrying around the base of the structure. The Commander decides that the party will investigate and you set off across the blue sands of the dry, hot planet.

As you approach you begin to establish more and more details. The metallic structure is a large steel block with no features interrupting its sheer silver sides. You estimate that it is about eight times the size of your spacecraft, which makes it nearly a hundred and fifty metres high.

The figures moving around its base are two-legged and look, in fact, not unlike humans, but are wearing blue robes and have a skin colour which is itself a deep, dark blue. By the time you are able to distinguish their facial features, they have noticed your approach. Their seemingly random movement around the base of the edifice ceases and they face you, carefully observing your approach. The Commander gives an order:

'Have your weapons ready, but try not to look threatening.'

You, along with the rest of the party, activate your laser pistol.

As you draw near to the figures, they begin to walk towards you but suddenly they stop, forming a perfectly straight line. You continue noting details to include in your report: the figures wear robes over skin-tight garments which seem to you to be made from some material resembling snake skin; you cannot tell whether the figures are male or female, as they all have equivalent facial features and all have dark, closely cropped hair; they seem to you to be identical, distinguishable only by the different designs they have tattooed on their cheeks, geometrical figures or swirls in dark red; and each has a long, cylindrical object secured to its back, protruding above the left shoulder.

The figures stand, unsmiling, showing no sign of welcome or fear. One, standing in the centre of the line, steps forward. Its robe is distinguished from the rest by a series of small patterns arranged down the front of the garment.

The figure stares directly at the party and in a sudden gesture, raises its arms above its head, maintaining eye-contact with you. A strange sound emerges from its lips, resembling no language you have ever heard. You cannot even decide whether it is, in fact, a language or merely a succession of noises. Its arms still raised above its head, the figure begins to sway and move in something resembling a dance. Its movement is fluid and beautiful. You notice that the creature is moving its feet in an elaborate pattern and, while watching the feet, you begin to discern the point of the movement: the figure is drawing, with its feet, an intricate design in the sand.

Slowly, as you watch a pattern emerges, you see that the figure is representing, in its sand-drawing, the spacecraft in which you arrived on the planet. The drawing is quite remarkably detailed and perfectly proportioned. As soon as the illustration is complete (the entire process takes a little over five minutes), the figure turns its back on you and faces the line of creatures who have remained stationary, staring straight ahead throughout the entire process. He utters, quietly but audibly, a series of sounds.

Suddenly the line moves. Simultaneously, each creature steps forward with its left foot and shoots its right arm over its left shoulder to grasp the protruding cylindrical object. Each withdraws the object from the harness on its back, and holds it in both hands, like one might hold a sword. The objects are cylindrical but sharpened; the sharp points pointing at your party are manufactured from a shining steel. Each creature begins to speak, or make noises, loudly: a series of harsh, short, sharp sounds.

The Commander is the first to panic and open fire. The bolt from his laser weapon surprises all of you, as though waking you from a dream. Other members of the party follow the Commander's example and let loose the deadly flashes of light. Five or six of the creatures are immediately thrown back onto the blue sand, one of them writhing in pain. Those still facing you seem at something of a loss as to what to do. None of them run away. Then those still standing run towards you. The contact does not last long: within minutes all of the creatures lie dead or dying on the sands of their planet.

The Commander, his authority established, orders the party to search the bodies and to collect samples of what the creatures are carrying or wearing, as well as samples of the blue sand of the planet. He does not wish to linger for fear that the death of these creatures might bring a larger, better-armed force.

You find several objects on the two bodies that you search: both creatures were carrying small pouches containing a quantity of sand indistinguishable from the sand of the surrounding desert; one of the bodies has a small brass tube tied to its belt which, on opening, you discover, contains three amber-coloured, smooth stones, and the other creature, hidden inside its robe, has a small model of a spacecraft, not unlike that in which you arrived. The Commander orders the giant metal structure to be searched, but no access to it can be discovered: it seems to be simply a giant block of highly polished steel.

Back aboard your spacecraft, the samples and artefacts are stored safely and the crew begins to discuss the encounter. They hold different views about the blue creatures you encountered: each seems to have his or her own interpretation of the species you confronted and the planet you were starting to explore.

The Commander does not see the encounter as a failure: The Company now knows of the existence of the planet and a quick analysis of the samples of blue sand suggests that the planet may be rich in lithium, a substance in demand on Earth for use in pharmaceuticals. The Company will be able to return with a larger military expedition – better informed following the discoveries you have made – to attempt to establish a mining and extracting operation. That night, having heard all of the opinions of the crew, you sit down to begin your report to The Company Directors.

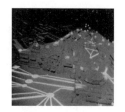

TIME OFF
TO WRITE!

Now you are going to write the report of your experiences for The Directors of The Company. You will probably find that your report is at least two pages long. It should not be longer than three pages because The Directors are busy people who do not take kindly to long reports. Below is a suggested scheme for the report. You don't need to follow it exactly, but you should cover all of the points it mentions. You may refer to the planet by the name coined on board ship after the encounter, 'Far Blue'.

EXPLORATION REPORT TO THE DIRECTORS: THE DISCOVERY OF 'FAR BLUE' (X1493)

Introduction:
- ❂ The reasons why you landed on the planet in the first place;
- ❂ the composition of the party; and
- ❂ the mood of the landing party (how they felt about what was occurring).

Paragraph 1
- ❂ Describe the appearance of the planet.

Paragraph 2
- ❂ Describe the appearance of the blue 'creatures'.

Paragraph 3
- ❂ Explain everything that happened before the first shot was fired.

Paragraph 4
- ❂ Suggest an interpretation of the dance.

Paragraph 5

❂ Describe the 'confrontation', defending the decision of the Commander to fire.

Paragraph 6

❂ List the things your party discovered on the bodies of the creatures.

Conclusion:

❂ Sum up your opinion of the creatures. (Are they an 'advanced' civilization? Are they violent? Will they be enemies or allies of Earth?)

❂ Advise The Directors on whether to proceed with mining operations on the planet and how to deal with the blue creatures.

Now think about the writing process you have just completed. Answer the following questions, in note form, thinking through the issues they raise.

❂ What difficulties did you experience in trying to interpret the dance?

❂ You had to write a defence of the Commander's actions in your report (given who the report is for and that the Commander will be the first to read it). Could you criticize his decision to fire? Make a recommendation as to whether or not you feel that The Company should discipline the Commander. On what basis could you do so?

❂ How much do you feel you learnt about the culture of the inhabitants of 'Far Blue'?

❂ Did you learn enough to make sensible suggestions as to how The Company should act towards the creatures in the future?

❂ Imagine an account by a blue creature who survives the encounter. How might her representation of the sequence of events differ from the way that you reported them?

Notice that your report is both an interpretation of the events that occurred (you have had to give the events meaning) and an evaluation (you have judged the culture of the blue creatures). Try to decide whether your interpretation and evaluation of the foreign culture is entirely in your own terms (whether you are interpreting them as if they are human, or whether you are constantly comparing them to human society).

2   Difficulties in representing others

When you wrote your report on 'Far Blue', you had to interpret aspects of another culture. You had to decide, from the evidence and your own knowledge of the world, what the significance of a range of things was in the context in which you encountered them. You had to think about the objects the creatures carried, the drawing in the sand, the raising of the 'weapons', the silver structure, the facial tattooing, and the utterances of the creatures. In other words, you had to offer an interpretation of another culture by deciding what all these things might mean. In the course of your interpretation, you had to work from the basis that:

✪ you did not understand the language of the culture
   you encountered;
✪ you knew nothing about the culture of the blue creatures
   that you could use to interpret their actions or objects;
✪ your interpretation was linked to who you are and to your
   background;
✪ your interpretation was affected by what you (as a character
   in the story) felt about 'aliens'; and
✪ your interpretation was affected by the objectives of
   The Company (since you were on the planet for a
   particular reason).

Let's look at some of the interpretative possibilities of just three of the things that you discussed in your report.

● SHOULD WE interpret one society (such as the one on 'Far Blue') in terms of another (in this instance, a society on Earth)?

THE APPEARANCE OF THE PLANET AND THE CREATURES

We often think of new things we encounter in terms of those things with which we are familiar. Perhaps this process is necessary to understanding anything that we confront. We encounter the world and understand other contexts with reference to our own context.

Of course, one danger of this tendency is that we may uncritically accept our context as normal, preferable and as the standard against which other contexts are to be judged. It is all very well to assert that others (other cultures, genders, individuals) are 'different from us'. However, if we see difference as deviation (difference from us), abnormality (assuming that 'we' are normal and other societies are not) or inferiority (seeing another society as less developed or less moral than our own), we run the risk of over-simplifying the factors that create difference. Similarly, we risk treating the people we consider different as less important than ourselves.

In the story about 'Far Blue', the colour of the sand is 'strange' because it is something with which we are not familiar. A society without clearly demarcated genders is 'unusual' because we are used to thinking of the world in terms of men and women. Red tattoos on blue faces are a 'deviation' from what we would expect because they do not exist in our culture. These examples illustrate that we tend to think comparatively: to compare what we encounter to our own cultural practices and characteristics. In language this is apparent in the process of representing others in our own terms. We use our way of describing the world to describe people or cultures who may have very different ways of understanding and describing their world.

THE DANCE, THE DRAWING AND THE POINTING OF THE WEAPONS

Because you know nothing of the cultural context of the society you confront, it is very difficult for you to interpret these three things. Since your 'first encounter' is so brief and incomplete, you cannot establish what meaning the blue creatures would give to each event. Since these actions could mean various things in different human societies, you might interpret them in many different ways. You have no basis for choosing between these competing interpretations. Or do you?

The dance and the drawing in the sand may be a ceremony of welcome or a suggestion that you 'leave right away in the way that you came'. A question that might have occurred to you is, 'How could the dancer have known so much about our ship?' Again, you could suggest various possibilities, but you cannot deduce a definite and correct answer. Notice that the Commander immediately interpreted the cylindrical objects as weapons and the act of pointing them as threatening. This interpretation is based on what they 'would be' on Earth and what brandishing them 'would mean' in our cultural context. They may, of course, be something altogether different (tools, ceremonial staffs, containers of ashes of ancestors or religious objects, to list a few possibilities). The act of pointing them may be something other than threatening (such as a tribute, or a ceremonial expression of a desire to protect you from other evil creatures on the planet, or a religious gesture which confers on you the protection of the culture's ancestors).

Return to your report and answer the following questions, this time in written form. The length of the answers will depend on your particular report, but try to write down all of the important points.

❂ Did you mention the dance in your report? Did you suggest that it meant anything in particular? What evidence did you use for your interpretation?

❂ Did you mention the drawing of the spacecraft in the sand? Did you suggest what it might mean?

❂ Why did you think the cylindrical objects were weapons?

❂ Looking at your answers to the previous three questions, how were your interpretations influenced by familiar objects/actions in your context?

❂ In what ways did you think of the planet and the creatures as 'strange' in comparison to Earth and human society?

❂ To what extent does your report reflect 'comparative thinking'?

❂ Did 'comparative thinking' cause you to misrepresent anything about the culture of the blue creatures?

Why would anyone, surrounded by blue sand, want to carry a small portion of it in a leather pouch? What could be the significance of three polished stones in a brass tube attached to a belt? Why would an adult carry, concealed in its robe, the model of a spacecraft? The meaning of these objects must reside in the meaning that they have for the individuals who carry them. For the interpreter from Earth, their meaning is completely unclear: we literally cannot interpret them from outside the culture which gives them certain meanings. We can suggest various possibilities as to what they might mean, but we cannot know which of them might be valid.

This may seem an obvious point: we could argue that there is a way to make a valid interpretation of the blue creatures' practices and artefacts. What blocks our interpretation is precisely our different context. In other words, our cultural background could distance us from what we are attempting to interpret. Dialogue between people of differing cultures could be one means of reducing that distance. In the case of 'Far Blue', the fact that you did not understand the language of the creatures and they did not understand yours is an obvious problem. But, in the long term, this lack of understanding is not necessarily insurmountable.

Representing others in language

The act of representing others, as you did in your report to The Directors of The Company, is usually a linguistic act (visual art and film imagery may be exceptions). In order to understand representation, we need to look carefully at the linguistic acts through which it is conducted. Before we leave the blue creatures, let's look at some of the issues surrounding the language of representation.

In the description you read of the encounter on 'Far Blue', the blue beings were frequently referred to as 'creatures'. The Oxford Advanced Learner's Dictionary defines 'creature' as:

creature /ˈkriːtʃə(r)/ *n* **1** a living being, esp an animal: *octopuses and other marine creatures* ○ *That dog's a ferocious creature!* ○ *strange creatures from Mars.* **2** (esp following an *adj*) a person, considered in a particular way: *She was a charming young creature.* ○ *a poor creature* (ie a person for whom one feels pity) ○ *It's 12.00, so he'll be at lunch now — he's*

The *Oxford English Dictionary* defines 'creature' in a way that is even more useful for our purposes:

Created thing; animate being; animal (often as distinct from man); human being, person (esp. w. term of admiration, contempt or patronage, etc.), one who owes his fortune to, and remains subservient to, another.

ADAPTED FROM: *Oxford English Dictionary*, p.1153. 1971. Oxford: Oxford University Press.

The connotations of referring to humans as 'creatures' are often negative, since the word is often used to denote the inhuman or animal as well. Secondly, the denotation that 'creatures' tend to be subservient, connotes their inferiority to us, to those we think of as 'human'. Simply by using the word 'creatures', given its connotations, we are passing judgement on the blue beings.

By defining the beings according to their colour, by referring to them as 'blue creatures', we are elevating their colour (because it is different from ours) to the position of their defining attribute or characteristic. In all likelihood, the race has a name or names by which it refers to itself. The best option for naming any culture (or subculture) would be to let it choose the name it prefers. Any name attached from outside a culture will tend to be judgemental, inaccurate or inadequate.

THE CREW SPEAKS

In the crew's discussion of the encounter on the planet, the following statements were made. Look carefully at the language and logic used in each case and judge whether you think it encourages or hinders cultural understanding. Assess, without having to answer in writing, whether each of the following statements seems to you to be evidence of an error or blindness on the part of the speaker.

- 'Imagine living in a society where you cannot tell men apart from women.'
- 'They have no sense of fashion if their haircuts are anything to go by.'
- 'At first I didn't think they would become so aggressive.'
- 'I don't think, by our standards, that they are very civilized.'
- 'The steel block must be of religious significance, like the Egyptian pyramids.'
- 'They were incredibly ugly.'
- 'That dance was pretty weird, if you ask me.'
- 'They seem to be very primitive: those robes looked medieval.'
- 'Their society must be a very simple and pure one. I'm sure they are very spiritual.'
- 'Clearly they are not using their lithium reserves, so we might as well.'

We now leave the blue planet, but the questions we have explored about the language and logic of representation will form the basis for the next section. The point to keep in mind throughout is that the way we describe other cultures frequently involves making judgements about them, and we often act on the basis of judgements we have made. For instance, your report to The Directors of The Company would be used to brief the next group travelling from Earth to 'Far Blue'. If you chose to represent the beings you encountered as cruel and uncivilized, or as violent savages, then this group would behave as if this is what they are. Their future as a civilization might depend on the way in which you have represented them in your report.

TIME OFF
TO THINK!

Can you think of any situation in human history that might have been, in any way, similar to the situation on 'Far Blue'?

. . . .

THREE

WRITING ABOUT OTHER CULTURES

IN THIS SECTION we will look at some of the difficulties of representing other cultures in writing. Although the representation of other cultures is a common and important aspect of much writing (think about journalism, for instance), it is also an aspect that needs to be approached with sensitivity and caution. Whether we are conscious of it or not, our representations of other cultures might be offensive or hurtful to the people who comprise that culture. More significantly, representations of groups of people can cause serious social conflict, particularly if they promote notions of superiority and inferiority, whether of culture, race, religion or gender. To explore some of these problems more closely we are going to look at colonialism, imperialism and writing.

1   Colonialism, imperialism and cultural domination

Marlow, the narrator in Joseph Conrad's *Heart of Darkness*, describes the practice of colonialism and imperialism in the nineteenth century as 'the conquest of the earth'. He says:

> The conquest of the earth, which mostly means taking it away from those who have a different complexion or slightly flatter noses than ourselves, is not a pretty thing when you look into it too much.

FROM: Joseph Conrad, *Heart of Darkness*, p. 8. Edited by Mitzi Anderson, Deirdre Byrne, and Michael Titlestad. 1998. Pretoria: UNISA Press.

- WHAT ACTIONS and ideas do you associate with the word 'colonialism'?

- HOW are the words 'colony' and 'colonial' usually used?

HEART OF DARKNESS, a novella (short novel) set in colonial Congo, was first published in *Blackwoods* Magazine in 1899. Its author, Joseph Conrad, had been employed by a company trading for ivory along the Congo River. At the time, the Congo was the personal property of King Leopold of Belgium, having been ceded to him at the Berlin Conference supposedly because of his intention to 'civilize' the Congolese and orchestrate their conversion to Christianity. The story is narrated by Marlow, who tells of his experiences as the captain of a steamboat sent up the river to fetch an ill company director who has begun to wield quite terrifying power over a local tribe. The director, Kurtz, has set himself up as a chief, but has, according to Marlow, claimed almost godlike status. The novella is Marlow's exploration of colonialism, both the reasons for its existence and the harsh realities that it involves.

King Leopold II of the Belgians

The 'conquest of the earth' refers to the colonization of various nations by European powers eager to gain new territories in order to boost their economic wealth and political power. It was during this period that the word 'imperialism' entered the English language. The word 'imperialist' was used before this, but it meant a supporter of an emperor or of the emperor's rule. The nineteenth-century concept of 'imperialism' referred to 'colonial trade or rule' (Raymond Williams, *Keywords*. 1983. London: Fontana). In this sense it referred to the imposition of European government in much of Africa, America and Asia, through which the people living there lost any independence and became subservient to the colonial powers in all respects. There were many forms of colonialism. Some were simply brutal exploitation and involved the destruction of cultures and peoples. Others were motivated by the belief that civilization and other 'benefits' were being brought to parts of the world that were undeveloped and primitive.

The idea of bringing civilization to undeveloped countries (the so-called 'civilizing mission') needs to be thought through carefully. Surely the colonies were already 'civilized', but simply according to different notions of civilization? Moreover, what gives one country the right to want to 'civilize' another? Finally, we need to ask what that 'civilizing' actually involved.

We tend now to think of colonialism in a more general sense than 'imperialism'. We think of it as a word describing the way one country or culture dominates another and uses it for its own purposes. It describes a relationship between two cultures based on an uneven distribution of power in which one culture takes on a role of 'master' and the other is forced into a subservient position.

Cultures have collided throughout history. Where those cultures have differed in military and technological capacity, the stronger of the two has often set itself up in a dominant position over the weaker. Many representations of cultures occur in colonial contexts, where one culture represents itself in a certain relationship to another, usually

THE PROCESS OF REPRESENTATION

In representing cultures they are named (and names are not necessarily neutral or innocent). As well as being named, cultures are defined according to the specific attributes the writer thinks they have. In the course of definition — which we can think of as the process of labelling different aspects of a culture — the culture is interpreted. Interpretation means that the writer who is representing the culture gives particular meanings to aspects of the culture and its practices.

as 'superior' in some way to the colonized culture, which it represents as 'inferior'.

While colonialism and imperialism are obviously harsh political realities, we can gain insight into them by looking at the language through which the cultures involved are represented. The process of naming, defining, interpreting and representing another culture is often the basis on which colonialism justifies its existence and manages to sustain itself.

Remember what is at stake. In writing or speaking about another culture, it is possible to create representations of it that make your domination of that culture seem both logical and appropriate. Often, too, people internalize these representations, and cultures become conditioned to accept their own alleged inferiority. Understanding how cultures are written about is so important because it determines the way in which they are perceived and, therefore, the way in which others treat them.

② Names and naming

To assess the effect of certain forms of naming in society, we can begin by looking at some examples. Let's look at three names that have been used to label cultures, one specific – 'Basarwa' – and the other two general – 'barbarian' and 'savage'.

The traditionally hunting and gathering tribes of Botswana and north-western South Africa are called, in Setswana, the Basarwa. This name is by no means neutral. In Tswana culture, which is dominant in the region,

LANGUAGE AND POWER

If language determines our interpretation of the world, then changing the language in which you represent it can change the way people think about the world. For instance, naming people in certain ways and describing them in particular terms can affect other people's reactions to them. Language can be seen as a primary means of wielding power.

Think, for example, about political speeches. Politicians try to influence the reactions of the population to whom they speak. They seek support for themselves and their policies. They achieve this support best by telling people what they want to hear, by reinforcing what people want to believe about the world. An important aspect of these beliefs is a people's view of their identity: who they are and what defines their culture. Much political language relates to this sense of identity and frequently functions through a process of naming and describing cultural 'others'. Societies often operate with a sense of their difference from others and this difference is represented (or even, some would say, is created) in language. Power and language are inseparably linked.

To understand how power operates in society we need to ask several questions:
- Who is given the right to speak (and write)?
- Whose speech is directly or indirectly silenced?
- How does that speech create the culture of the speaker?
- How does that speech represent other cultures or aspects of other cultures?
- Does the language take anything for granted about the 'correctness' of its representations?
- Who is given the power to speak for other people or, stated differently, who does a society regard as experts in any aspect of the culture?

cattle ownership is an indication of wealth, social status and success. Those who do not own cattle are considered to be inadequate, as outside of the society and lacking in power and influence. 'Basarwa' means 'those who do not own cattle' and, while this may seem to simply describe the lifestyle of the tribes it names, it has strongly negative connotations and is an expression of the prevailing racism against the tribes. An organization formed by the tribes, 'First People', has been faced with a crisis of naming: clearly the name 'Basarwa' is unacceptable, but the tribes have never needed to refer to themselves collectively, they have always named themselves as individual communities: /Gwi, !Kung and so on. In order to combat the racism to which they are subjected they require a unified identity and, therefore, a name. 'First People' have decided to choose the term 'Bushmen', a colonial name that is, on many levels, equally unacceptable. The motive for selecting it is that it avoids the connotations of 'Basarwa' and is at least known in European countries to whom they are appealing for assistance.

The term 'barbarian' was first used in the English language, as far as we know, in 1549. The word, though, has a far longer history; it existed in ancient Greek (barbaros), Latin (barbarus) and Old French (barbarien). The word has always been used to refer to foreigners in different cultures: non-Romans, non-Christians and non-Italians, among others. It has always had the sense of 'those who have a rude language', the implication being that 'they' are inferior because they do not speak Latin, French, Italian or English, depending on who is using the word. By 1613, the word meant 'wild and uncivilized' and had become a synonym for 'savage' (which also had the sense of 'being in a state of nature'). When a member of another culture is labelled a 'barbarian' or a 'savage', a strong judgement is implied: the culture of which he or she is a member is seen as no culture at all, but a wild and uncivilized group of people lacking the basic characteristics that define human society.

A useful illustration of the connotations of the word 'barbarian' is a description of 'barbarians' in a contemporary South African novel. The novel, *Waiting for the Barbarians* by J. M. Coetzee, describes a colonial context in which a fictitious 'Empire' represents itself as under threat from 'barbarians', who are the nomadic tribes whose territory the Empire's soldiers have invaded. In order to criticize imperial discourse, Coetzee uses the language that colonial powers employed to describe the cultures they encountered. The following extract from *Waiting for the Barbarians* describes the thoughts of the Magistrate, the main character and narrator, who has begun to wonder about the truth of the Empire's propaganda about the 'barbarians'.

Y LAST YEAR STORIES had begun to reach us from the capital of unrest among the barbarians. Traders travelling safe routes had been attacked and plundered. Stock thefts had increased in scale and audacity. A party of census officials had disappeared and been found in shallow graves. Shots had been fired at a provincial governor during a tour of inspection. There had been clashes with border patrols. The barbarian tribes were arming, the rumour went; the Empire should take precautionary measures, for there would certainly be war.

Of this unrest I myself saw nothing. In private I observed that once in every generation, without fail, there is an episode of hysteria about the barbarians. There is no woman living along the frontier who has not dreamed of a dark barbarian hand coming from under her bed to grip her ankle, no man who has not frightened himself with visions of barbarians carousing in his home, breaking the plates, raping his daughters.

FROM: J. M. Coetzee, *Waiting for the Barbarians*,
p. 8. 1980. London: Martin Secker and Warburg.

Answer the following questions about this extract:
✪ How does the society characterize the 'barbarians'? (Look at the way their behaviour is described by the Magistrate.)
✪ If this view of the 'barbarians' was true, would the Empire be justified in treating them harshly and controlling them?

- What is the significance of the Magistrate stating that he has never seen the reported unrest?
- In what way might the rulers of the Empire be using the 'barbarian threat' to serve their own purposes?

Let's return to the word 'savage' for a moment. At times in its history it has had the connotation of 'living in a state of nature'. This led certain European thinkers in the eighteenth century (such as Rousseau and Montaigne) to link the concepts of 'noble' and of 'savage'. To them, the 'noble savage' represented an innocent and uncorrupted state of humanity before it was destroyed by political oppression and the social complexities of European society. While this could be considered complimentary on one level, it must be remembered that the concept of the 'noble savage' was based on the idea that black Africans lived in a state of childlike simplicity, since the term had connotations of 'naïveté' and 'underdevelopment'. The concept suggested that Europeans had become corrupted, but that Africans had not yet 'developed' far enough to have suffered that corruption.

These examples illustrate that the names by which we refer to others, as individuals or as a culture, might not be neutral labels, but could be explicit or implied judgements of them. It is useful to ask the following questions of names of cultures, races or societies:
- From what other words, and with what connotations, does the name originate?
- Who chose the name (the culture itself or some other group)?
- What does the name mean in current usage (what are its denotations and connotations)?
- When was the name chosen and for what specific reasons?

SOMETHING

TO THINK ABOUT!

If you had to suggest a policy for deciding which names are acceptable for a culture and which not, what would that policy be?

③ Generalizations

Names for cultures are essential in any discourse° about societies and individuals. We cannot speak about a culture without naming it. Names, though, often imply judgements about a culture. Names of societies are also used in statements that generalize about a culture. The very fact that a culture is referred to as having a collective identity means that it becomes possible to overlook the complex contradictions and differences within culture. Imagine a culture named the 'troggles'. As soon as we begin to say things such as, 'All troggles believe in marriage,' we have entered the field of generalization.

Look at the following statements, all of which are generalizations, and assess whether you think they are valid or not. Give reasons for your decision in each case.

- ✪ 'All Germans are very precise and hard-working.'
- ✪ 'Italians are incredibly talkative.'
- ✪ 'White people can't dance.'
- ✪ 'Black students are less successful academically than white students.'
- ✪ 'All Aborigines have a right to ancestral land.'
- ✪ 'Japanese men make the most significant decisions in the world economy.'
- ✪ 'Black people can't swim.'
- ✪ 'The Bushmen suffer from various forms of oppression.'

Each of these statements has to be considered on its own merits. Certain forms of generalization are essential in discussing culture, and often generalization is a valid and necessary practice. It is necessary if we decide that we need to think of cultures as having a unique set of priorities and as having a right to their own identity. It is also valid for a culture to use generalizations if it seeks a unified identity for some political purpose. It ceases to be valid, and becomes objectionable, when the generalizations are racist. Because we are concerned here with cultural difference, rather than gender or other differences, the generalizations that we are concerned with are those concerning culture. Other forms of generalization can be equally detrimental.

Racism has two aspects: firstly, it generalizes about a specific culture, and secondly, it links human abilities and capacities to race, defining some races as superior to others. Whenever you encounter the names of cultures, you should assess the statements in which they are used to see whether they have racist implications or not.

SOMETHING
TO DO!

Select six statements that you have heard about cultures in your own country that rely on generalizations. Then decide whether or not each of the statements is racist.

Statement based on generalization	Racist	Non-racist

Another practice in the naming of cultures of which we should remain aware is the use of the third-person plural pronoun 'they' and its variants ('them' and 'their'). This word, too, involves a process of generalization. Any statement that describes people *en masse* (not seeing them as individuals with differences) and attributes particular characteristics to them is potentially racist. As with many other linguistic practices, there is more to the process of generalization than may first seem to be the case. As soon as we stop thinking and speaking of cultures as comprised of different individuals, we make it possible to treat members of that culture as though they are not individual human beings. Given the connection between language and reality, the way we speak of the world determines how we understand it and how we behave in it. Racism in language, therefore, is not simply a linguistic issue.

An example of such racist generalization, one that had appalling consequences, was Nazi anti-Semitism. Jews in Nazi propaganda were represented as a collective, undifferentiated mass of superstitious, alien and grotesque people. 'They' were shown in Nazi propaganda films intercut with images of swarming insects and rats. By extension, the Nazis were suggesting that 'they' (Jews) were inhuman and should be exterminated like insects and rats. Racist colonial representations of African tribes by colonial writers created myths based on stereotypes defined by very similar characteristics. Stereotyping often precedes racist conduct; in the case of the Jews, it contributed to the Holocaust, in which over six million people were killed in Nazi death camps. History constantly reveals the appalling effects of generalizing, dehumanizing and stereotyping cultures or people. To be aware of these processes may be one way of preventing them from having the terrible effects they have had in the past.

 Interpretations

We have already spoken about how the cultural and personal contexts from which we come influence how we interpret and judge whatever we encounter. As a result, the same event, practice or object can be interpreted in entirely different ways by individuals from different contexts. This occurs because the context from which we come gives us a frame of reference from within which we give meaning to the world. When we interpret, we usually relate the new to that with which we are familiar. Remember, too, if in your culture something has always been interpreted in certain ways, these interpretations will affect how you understand it. For example, if certain groups of people have always been thought of as inferior, then your interpretation of them will be affected by previous interpretations.

TIME FOR
A COLONIAL ENCOUNTER!

Next you'll read two descriptions of the same event, a meeting between two groups who have never encountered each other before. The context is the Congo at the time when it was under the colonial rule of King Leopold (the era Joseph Conrad writes about in *Heart of Darkness*). The first passage is adapted from the writings of the explorer Henry Morton Stanley. The second passage is adapted from an oral account of the same encounter by a tribal chief whose people were attacked by Stanley's expeditionary force.

People such as Stanley explored areas of the Congo that were unfamiliar to Europeans, although once they had completed their explorations, other Europeans frequently ventured into the areas they described. For instance, agents of King Leopold moved into the areas first described by Stanley and exploited the inhabitants of those areas in the various brutal ways they 'traded' with them for rubber and ivory. The Congo was also being used, though unofficially, as a source of slaves for various enterprises of the colonists.

That was no welcome!

ABOUT 8 A.M. we came in view of the marketplace, near which there were many small canoes. The men at once rushed into them and advanced all round us. We held back for a long time, but finally, they became emboldened by our stillness and began to launch their wooden spears, which they proceeded to do all together as soon as someone cried out 'Mutt' (sticks). At that point, we were obliged to reply to them with a few shots, which compelled them to scamper away ahead of us. Drums then awakened the whole country and horns blew deafening blasts. Some canoes boldly followed us.

III. The Belgian Congo

WE CAME ABOUT 10 A.M., to another market green. Here too warriors were ready, and again we used our weapons. The little canoes with loud threats disappeared quickly down river: the land warriors rushed away into the woods. We did not wish to hurry, because the faster we proceeded the quicker we found we were involved in trouble. We therefore loitered indifferently: rest was so rare that it became precious when we obtained it.

AT 2 P.M. we emerged out of the shelter into the deeply wooded banks and came into the vast stream, nearly 2 000 yards across at the mouth. As soon as we entered into waters, we saw a great fleet of canoes hovering about in the middle of the stream. The canoe men, standing up, gave a loud shout when they saw us and blew their horns louder than ever. We pulled briskly on to gain the right bank when, looking upstream, we saw a sight that sent the blood tingling through every nerve and fibre of our bodies: a flotilla of gigantic canoes bearing down on us, which both in size and numbers greatly exceeded anything we had seen hitherto!

Instead of aiming for the right bank, we kept straight down river, the boat taking position behind. Yet after a moment's reflection, as I noted the numbers of the savages, the daring manner of the pursuit, and the apparent desire of our canoes to abandon the steady compact line, I gave the order to drop anchor. Four of our canoes made believe not to listen, until I chased them to return to the line, which was formed of eleven double canoes, anchored ten yards apart. The boat moved up to the front and took position fifty yards above them. The shields were next lifted by the noncombatants, men, women and children in the bows, and along the outer lines, as well as astern, and from behind these the muskets and rifles were aimed.

We had sufficient time to take a view of the mighty force bearing down on us and to count the number of war vessels. There were fifty-four of them! A monster canoe led the way, with two rows of upstanding paddles, forty men on a side, their bodies bending and swaying in unison as with a swelling barbarous chorus they drove her down toward us.

In the bow, standing on what appeared to be a platform, were ten prime young warriors, their heads gay with red feathers: at the stern, eight men with long paddles, whose tops were decorated with ivory balls, guided the monster vessel; and dancing up and down from stern to stern were ten men who appeared to be chiefs.

THE CRASHING SOUND OF LARGE DRUMS, a hundred blasts from ivory horns, and a thrilling chant from 2 000 human throats did not tend to soothe our nerves or to increase our confidence. However, it was 'neck or nothing'. We had no time to pray or take sentimental looks at the savage world, or even to breathe a sad farewell to it. So many other things had to be done speedily and well.

As the first canoe came rushing down, its consorts on either side beating the water into foam and raising their jets of water with their sharp prows, I turned to take a last look at our people and said to them: 'Boys, be firm as iron; wait until you see the first spear, and then take good aim. Don't fire all at once. Keep aiming until you are sure of your man. Don't think of running away, for only your guns can save you.'

THE MONSTER CANOE aimed straight for my boat, as though it would run us down! Then it swerved aside and when nearly opposite, the warriors above the manned prow let fly their spears and on either side there was a noise of rushing bodies. But every sound was soon lost in the ripping, crackling musketry. For five minutes we were so absorbed in firing that we took no note of anything else; but at the end of that time we were made aware that the enemy was re-forming about 200 yards above us.

OUR BLOOD WAS UP NOW. It was a murderous world, and we felt for the first time that we hated the filthy, vulturous ghouls who inhabited it. We therefore lifted our anchors and pursued them upstream along the right river bank until, rounding a point, we saw their villages. We made straight for the banks and continued the fight in the village streets with those who had landed. We hunted them out into the woods, and only sounded the retreat after we had returned the daring cannibals the compliment of a visit.

BASED ON: Henry Morton Stanley, *The Congo and the Founding of its Free State: A Story of Work and Exploration.* 1885. London: Sampson Low, Marston, Searle and Rivington.

That was no brother!

WHEN WE HEARD that the man with the white flesh was journeying down the Lualaba (Congo) River we were open-mouthed with astonishment. We stood still. All night long the drums announced the strange news – a man with white flesh! That man, we said to ourselves, has a white skin. He must have got that from the river kingdom. He will be one of our brothers who were drowned in the river. All life comes from the water, and in the water he has found life. Now he is coming back to us, he is coming home...

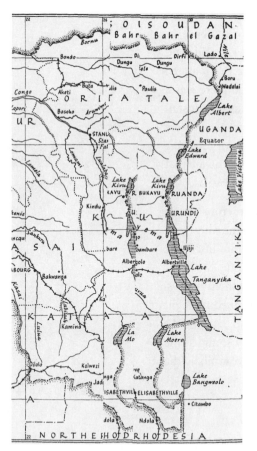

WE WILL PREPARE A FEAST, I ordered, we will go to meet our brother and escort him into the village with rejoicing! We dressed in our ceremonial clothes. We assembled the great canoes. We listened for the gong which would announce our brother's presence on the Lualaba. Presently the cry was heard: He is approaching the Lohali! Now he enters the river! Halloh! We swept forward, my canoe leading, the others following, with songs of joy and dancing, to meet the first white man our eyes had beheld, and to do him honour.

BUT AS WE DREW NEAR HIS CANOES there were loud, explosive sounds, bang! bang! and fire sticks spat bits of iron at us. We were paralysed with fright: our mouths hung wide open and we could not shut them. Things such as we had never seen, never heard of, never dreamed of – they were the work of evil spirits!

SEVERAL OF MY MEN plunged into the water ... What for? Did they fly to safety? No, for others fell down also, in the canoes. Some screamed dreadfully, others were silent – they were dead, and blood flowed from little holes in their bodies. 'War! That is war!' I yelled. 'Go back!' The canoes sped back to our village with all the strength our spirits could impart to our arms.

THAT WAS NO BROTHER! That was the worst enemy our country had ever seen.

And still those bangs went on: the long staves spat fire, flying pieces of iron whistled around us, fell into the water with a hissing sound, and our brothers continued to fall. We fled into our village – they came after us. We fled into the forest and flung ourselves on the ground. When we returned that evening our eyes beheld fearful things: our brothers, dead, bleeding, our village plundered and burned, and the water full of dead bodies.

The robbers and murderers had disappeared.

NOW TELL ME: has the white man dealt fairly by us? Oh, do not speak to me of him! You call us wicked men, but you white men are much more wicked! You think because you have guns you can take away our land and our possessions. You have sickness in your heads, for that is not justice.

> BASED ON: Richard Harding Davis,
> *The Congo and the Coasts of Africa.*
> 1907. New York: Scribner's.

Read the two passages ('That was no welcome!' and 'That was no brother!') again and then answer the following questions. You may find that you will need to return to the passages several times to find particular details to which you will refer in your answers.

✪ Do the facts given in the two accounts differ in any way?
How does Stanley interpret the clothing and the actions of the tribesmen?

❂ What were the consequences of Stanley's interpretation?

❂ What were the consequences of Stanley's interpretation?
❂ What did the tribesmen 'mean' by dressing and behaving as they did?
❂ Do you believe that Stanley's men fired after being attacked?

DO CULTURES differ much in what they believe is right and wrong? If we believe that definitions of right and wrong vary because of cultural context, how would this belief affect the way we think about other people? Are there any dangers in such a belief?

People interpret individual aspects of a culture differently, but they also interpret conflicts between cultures in different ways. These different interpretations depend on the value judgements made about the cultures involved. As we mentioned earlier in this section, the colonization of the Congo was a brutal process described by the novelist Joseph Conrad as 'robbery with violence'. Different people, though, represented the colonization in different ways. What follows are three different views of the colonization of the Congo. As you read them, think about the ways the writers represent the Congolese cultures.

EXTRACTS
TO READ!

Leopold speaks

LEOPOLD was the king of Belgium. The colony of the Congo was ceded to him as his private property by other European powers. Pretending to act in the best interests of the colony, Leopold established a series of companies, trading in rubber and ivory, which he used to amass a large personal fortune.

THE MISSION which the agents of the State have to accomplish on the Congo is a noble one. They have to continue the development of civilisation in the centre of Equatorial Africa, receiving their inspiration directly from Berlin and Brussels. Placed face to face with primitive barbarism, grasping with sanguinary customs that date back thousands of years, they are obliged to reduce these gradually. They must accustom the population to general laws, of which the most needful and salutary is assuredly that of work.

FROM: Robert Kimbrough (ed.), *Heart of Darkness*, Norton Critical Edition, p. 79. 1988. New York: N. W. Norton & Company.

WRITING WORLDS APART

Stanley supports the Belgian king

WHO CAN DOUBT that God chose the King for his instrument to redeem this vast slave park ... King Leopold found the Congo cursed by cannibalism, savagery and despair; and he has been trying with a patience, which I can never sufficiently admire; to relieve it of its horrors, rescue it from its oppressors, and save it from perdition.

ADAPTED FROM: Henry Morton Stanley, *The Congo and the Founding of its Free State: A Story of Work and Exploration.* 1885. London: Sampson Low, Marston, Searle and Rivington.

HENRY MORTON STANLEY was an American explorer and journalist who visited the Congo and, at first, praised and defended the actions of Leopold's company officials. His opinion changed slightly in the course of his career, but this passage is a typical example of attempts to defend Leopold's government.

But Davis disagrees

ATROCITIES HERE WERE OPEN and above-board ... In the opinion of the State, the soldiers, in killing game for food, wasted the State cartridges, and in consequence the soldiers, to show that they did not expend their cartridges extravagantly on antelope and wild boar, for each empty cartridge brought in a human hand, the hand of a man, woman, or child. These hands, drying in the sun, could be seen at the posts along the river. They are no longer in evidence. Neither is the flower bed of Lieutenant Dom, which was bordered with human skulls. A quaint conceit.

The man to blame for these atrocities, for each separate atrocity, is Leopold.

ADAPTED FROM: Richard Harding Davis, *The Congo and the Coasts of Africa.* 1907. New York: Scribner's.

RICHARD HARDING DAVIS was a journalist and missionary who attempted (along with many other writers) to reveal to the world the true nature of Leopold's exploitative and vicious government of the Congo.

● WHAT ARE your
personal feelings
about colonization?

Colonization is open to different interpretations. The views expressed in the extracts all rest on an interpretation and evaluation of the cultures and events involved in the colonization of the Congo.

Write a short piece (of about a page) in which you express how you feel about colonization. This is an exercise in which you will explore your personal opinions, but you should still give evidence and support for the points you make. In writing, it may be necessary for us to defend even our personal beliefs. Your evidence in this exercise could be personal stories or anecdotes that help explain why you hold the opinion that you do. Whatever evidence you use, you should make it clear to your reader both what you believe and why you hold those beliefs.

You could use these questions as a starting point to focus your mind on the issue:

✪ Has the country in which you live ever been colonized?
  If not, which ex-colonies do you know about?
✪ Did the colonization of your country (or the one you are thinking of) affect all people equally?
✪ Did colonization bring any good things to the country you are considering?
✪ What obviously bad things were a result of colonization?
✪ Are there any long-lasting effects of colonization?
✪ How might a country deal with its colonial past?

 Projections

A feature of the process of representing other cultures (naming, interpreting and comparing) is that one culture often uses another as a screen onto which it projects its own fears and desires. This is a complex concept. The idea is that, just as the sailor and camel-driver saw what they most wanted in the outline of Despina, so we often see in other cultures what we most desire. Alternatively, we might use them as representatives of our fears.

If you think back to J. M. Coetzee's 'barbarians', they are clearly an embodiment of the general fears and insecurities among the citizens of the Empire. What they are in reality (peaceful nomadic tribes) is not the way that they are perceived; they are perceived rather as imaginary projections of the Empire. The Empire, if you like, has created the barbarians in the mind of the public as representing all of the worst things it can imagine. In *Waiting for the Barbarians*, the State promotes and then uses the 'barbarian threat' to control the population, because by manipulating perceptions of the nomadic tribes they have a way of controlling and manipulating the fears of the population.

Many representations have more to do with the fears and desires of the representing culture than the culture being depicted. What we see in the world is often a result of what we want to see and of our fears about the world. The fact that 'other' cultures exist at a distance gives the representing culture a degree of freedom to express its innermost desires and fears in a way that cannot be achieved within their own culture. Others become something not, in any real sense, interpreted, but merely a site within which a culture reflects its own complexities and contradictions. In interpreting, we bring our own culture to bear on another. For this reason, the interpretation might say more about 'us' than it says about 'them'. This is an important issue to think about. Perhaps the way that we perceive (and represent) others is always a matter of the way that we perceive ourselves. It would be possible to argue that the 'other' is always a part of the 'self'.

A few points deserve consideration before the end of this chapter. It is difficult to avoid generalizations when we write about culture and the ways in which people interpret cultural difference. It is easy to fall into the trap of writing about colonialism as if it is always the same thing. Similarly, we tend to label all forms of racism as if they are alike. Think about the following five statements in light of all that you have explored in this chapter:

✪ Not all forms of racism are alike.
✪ Not all forms of colonialism or colonial practice are the same.
✪ Representations of a culture are seldom simplistically racist.
✪ We need to analyse representations carefully to determine the extent to which they are accurate, sympathetic and/or racist.
✪ We should never leap to conclusions in the analysis of culture.

Ending our journey: conclusion

A S YOU HAVE SEEN, people approach language and texts from many perspectives. On the basis of those perspectives and interests, they ask different questions about what they read. The four stages of our journey in this book have marked four such areas of interest in literary studies. We began by investigating 'the self' and progressed through a study of characterization to explore representations of gender and cultural difference. These areas of interest relate to the stories we tell and the language we use in representation.

The stories we tell about who we are and who other people are, and the language in which those stories are formulated, provide a useful base for thinking about the various kinds of texts we read. We hope that the ways we have discussed these issues here will make them accessible and interesting, and that they will help you as you explore the ways we think and write about ourselves and about others.

Glossary

arbitrary based on a decision or opinion, not on a certain system or for a specific reason.

assumption an idea or theory which someone holds without proof that it is true or accurate.

audience receivers of meaning.

bias an opinion or feeling that favours one side in an argument or one thing in a group often unfairly.

category a group whose parts share a common characteristic.

communication an event in which meaning is conveyed and received.

complexities the closely inter-related aspects and mutually influencing factors that combine to form a whole, be that whole a person, an object, an organization or an activity.

connotations the ideas and feelings that we associate with a word. Contrast with denotation, below. Both connotation and denotation are discussed in more detail in chapter four.

concept a complex idea or notion.

conditioned trained to behave in a certain way.

context the circumstances in which something happens and in which we see them.

convention an agreement about the way in which something is usually done; behaviour that is generally expected from people in a certain situation.

critically in common language, 'critical' is often used in the sense of 'thinking badly or poorly of something'. However, in English studies, we use 'critical' and 'critically' in the sense of thinking carefully and analytically about something or a text. 'Critical analysis' involves studying a text to discover how meaning is conveyed.

denotation the core or main meaning of a word, usually supplied first in a dictionary definition.

discourse a communication in speech or writing. In English studies, this term is also use to refer to the special terms, words, conventions and codes that provide the context of a communication. We might refer, for example, to academic discourse, feminist discourse or post-colonial discourse.

double standards a rule or principle that is applied strictly to one situation, person or group, but not to another.

extract a piece of writing selected from a larger text.

figurative language is used to imaginative effect, asking the reader to imagine a number of mental images or ideas. Contrast with literal, below, and *see connotation*.

implications things that are involved in or might result from something else or are suggested by something, but not directly stated.

impression collection of feelings or ideas.

infer reach an opinion based on given information or evidence.

intention purpose, reason.

linguistic formed by language.

literal the standard, or dictionary, meaning of a term (contrast with figurative, above). *See also denotation.*

objective means a viewpoint not affected by personal taste or attitudes, something real and accurate.

perspective point of view; the attitude you have towards something.

polemical means a viewpoint put forward very strongly, particularly when other people might disagree.

prejudice a feeling of dislike towards a person or group that is based on false information rather than real experiences.

process a series of activities undertaken in order to produce a result.

self-reflection thinking deeply and carefully about yourself.

significance important meaning or implication.

socialize to make somebody behave in ways that society accepts.

stereotype a fixed idea or

opinion about a type of
person, which is often not
true or accurate.

strategy a way of getting
something done.

subject can be used in
different ways. 'Subject'
is used in the context of
grammar and refers to the
word or phrase in a sentence
which indicates who or
what does the action stated
by the verb. It can also be
used in the same sense as
'topic'. However, 'subject' is
also increasingly used as a
synonym for 'the self'.

subjective means a viewpoint
which is affected by personal taste or attitudes.

text usually, a piece of writing.
However, recently this word
has also been used very
broadly to describe any
event that conveys
meaning.

world-view a particular way of
thinking about or seeing
people and the world that is
influenced by our upbring-
ing, education, experience,
beliefs and culture.

Copyright acknowledgements

THE PUBLISHERS AND AUTHORS would like to thank these individuals and organizations for providing material and granting permission for reproduction of both photographic and textual material.

Every effort has been made to trace copyright holders. Should any infringements have occurred, the publishers would be very grateful for information that will enable them to correct these in the event of a reprint.

COVER IMAGES: Head: The Image Bank, Joe Saffold; Leopold: frontispiece to George Matelli, *Leopold to Lumumba: A History of the Belgian Congo 1877–1960*, London: Chapman and Hall Ltd.; Map: George Matelli, *Leopold to Lumumba: A History of the Belgian Congo 1877–1960*, London: Chapman and Hall Ltd., p. 232; Nelson Mandela and Ruth First: Bailey's African Photo Archives, Bob Gosani; Figure in space: The Image Bank, Kevin Mayes.

PHOTOGRAPHS AND IMAGES: p. 31 Nelson Mandela and Ruth First: Bailey's African Photo Archives, Bob Gosani; Mandela singing with supporters, Bailey's African Photo Archives, Peter Magubane; Mandela pensive, the *Argus*; p. 41 ANC campaign stickers: courtesy the *Argus* archives; p. 52 Military vehicle with passing group: the *Argus*; p. 53 Funeral watched by security police: the *Argus*; children's march, the *Star*; Mandela (twice), the *Argus*; p. 79 Sophiatown: Mayibuye Centre, University of the Western Cape; pp. 120–121 Jane Austen advert: supplied by The Jupiter Drawing Room; p. 145 Map of present-day Gauteng: *New Oxford Atlas* Revised Edition, 1978, Oxford: Oxford University Press; pp. 183 and 189 Space ship: The Image Bank, Eic Meola Studio Inc.; p. 197 Leopold: frontispiece to George Matelli, *Leopold to Lumumba: A History of the Belgian Congo 1877–1960*, London: Chapman and Hall Ltd.; p. 207 and 210 Map: George Matelli, *Leopold to Lumumba: A History of the Belgian Congo 1877–1960*, London: Chapman and Hall Ltd., p. 232.

TEXT: p. 1 (right) Gloria Gaynor, 'I am what I am', Long Island Music Company Ltd; p. 16 from *The Metamorphosis* by Franz Kafka,

Index

reading skills, 32, 77–8, 96–103

Readings

Alice's Adventures in Wonderland, by Lewis Carroll, 14–15

Chronicle of a Death Foretold, by Gabriel Garcia Márquez, 159–62

The Congo and the Coasts of Africa, by R. H. Davis, 210–11 & map, 213

The Congo and the Founding of its Free State, by Henry Morton Stanley, 206–9 & map, 213

The Diving Bell and the Butterfly, by Jean Dominique Bauby, 42

Education for Marriage, by Estelle Cole, 117

A first encounter, 183–9

Gender and 'History': 1980s South African women's stories in English, by Margaret Daymond, 154–5

Heart of Darkness, by Joseph Conrad, 197, 212

Invisible Cities, by Italo Calvino, 168–9

The Life and Opinions of Tristram Shandy, by Laurence Sterne, 76

Long Walk to Freedom, by Nelson R.

Mandela, 26–31 & ill., 33–9, 41–4

Madam & Eve cartoon, 55

Man of the Year articles, TIME (magazine), 70–5

The Metamorphosis, by Franz Kafka, 16

Midnight's Children, by Salman Rushdie, 76

Pride and Prejudice, by Jane Austen, 157–9

Snow Falling on Cedars, by David Guterson, 104–5

The Suit, by Can Themba, 77–95

The Toilet, by Gcina Mhlope, 145–55

Waiting for the Barbarians, by J. M. Coetzee, 201

Writing a Woman's Life, by Carolyn G Heilbrun, 142–3

You are what you say, by Robin Lakoff, 132–6

report writing, 189–90

representation in writing, 3, 47, 70–5, 191–6

language use, 194–8

sexual difference, 114–17

role play, 126–31

Rushdie, Salman

Midnight's Children, 76

S

self, 5–9, 17, 76

sentence construction, 6–7

sexual difference, 114–15

sexuality, 115–16

societies, see culture

Sophiatown, 79 & ill.

space, 141, 143–4

Stanley, Henry Morton

The Congo and the Founding of its Free State, 206–9 & map, 213

stereotypes, 23, 57, 121, 177

Sterne, Laurence

The Life and Opinions of Tristram Shandy, 76

storytelling, 47–8, 54

see also narration

T

Themba, Can, 79

The Suit, 77, 80–95

TIME (magazine)

Man of the Year articles, 70–5

time lines, 51–4

tolerance, 175

translation

concepts, 178–80

connotation and denotation, 180, 182–3

V

values, 58

W

women

gender stereotypes,